The Second Decade of Love

Greg Johnson & Mike Yorkey

THE SECOND DECADE OF LOVE

Tyndale House Publishers, Inc.

WHEATON, ILLINOIS

All Scripture quotations, unless indicated, are taken from the *Holy Bible,* New International Version®. Copyright © 1973, 1978, 1984 by International Bible Society. Used by permission of Zondervan Publishing House. All rights reserved. The "NIV" and "New International Version" trademarks are registered in the United States Patent and Trademark Office by International Bible Society. Use of either trademark requires permission of International Bible Society.

Scripture quotations marked KJV are taken from the *Holy Bible,* King James Version.

Library of Congress Cataloging-in-Publication Data

Johnson, Greg,   date
   The second decade of love : finding a renaissance in marriage
before the kids leave home / Greg Johnson and Mike Yorkey.
      p.   cm.
   ISBN 0-8423-5919-2 (hardcover)
   1. Marriage—United States.   2. Marriage—Religious aspects—
Christianity.   I. Yorkey, Mike   II. Title.
HQ536.J65   1994   94-12492
306.81′0973—dc20

Printed in the United States of America

00   99   98   97   96   95   94
7   6   5   4   3   2   1

To Elaine . . .
From high school sweethearts, to young marrieds,
to young parents—eighteen years!
I can't wait for the next thirty!
—Greg

To Nicole . . .
The highs have always outweighed the lows.
—Mike

CONTENTS

FOREWORD

*m*any years ago, I sat down to talk with an attractive woman who was in obvious pain. With tears streaming down her face, she sobbed, "I've tried to express what's wrong in our marriage, but I just can't seem to explain it. What's the use of bringing it all up again?"

This woman had nearly given up hope of experiencing a loving, healthy, and lasting relationship with her husband. She had resigned herself to a marriage that fell far short of the wishes and dreams she had once had.

As a young family counselor, I had heard this kind of story before. I had spent countless hours talking with husbands and wives, helping to improve their relationship. Only now I wasn't sitting in a counseling office. I was seated at a kitchen table. And the woman sitting across from me was my own wife, Norma.

Our marriage was in the Dark Ages—a state you will hear more about in *The Second Decade of Love*. That day I made a decision to understand what was happening—and not happening—in my marriage. I also decided to find the answers to several important questions. Why was Norma feeling so frustrated in her attempts to communicate with me? Why did I have such a difficult time sharing my feelings with her? And why was it a struggle to understand each other—particularly when we discussed important issues?

It was a long journey for Norma and me to get back on track, but once we did, we began to experience a Renaissance in our marriage. I wish I had had this resource before I sat across from her that fateful afternoon.

Gary Smalley

ACKNOWLEDGMENTS

*t*o the dozens of couples who shared their happiness and heartbreaks, their ideas and their intimacies—we are deeply indebted. Without your honesty, all we'd have to talk about is our own marriages, and that wouldn't have been enough!

To Sandra Aldrich, thank you for editing our first manuscript. Your wonderful suggestions helped us improve the book. And to Bob Newman and Craig Torstenbo, thanks for your assistance with the Top Ten lists. You guys are hilarious!

*W*hen we told our wives we were going to write a book on marriage, they started laughing. *You've got to be kidding! Since when did you two become experts on marriage?*

Then we had another idea. *They* could write this book based on all the marital miscues they witnessed over the years. The publisher, however, took pity on them, so we got the call. After all, we were the ones who really needed the help.

The first thing we asked ourselves was this: Since there are already a bazillion books on marriage, how could this one be different?

Eureka! Let's write a book for couples in the eight- to twenty-year range of marriage—just like us. Let's write something *we* would want to read and include humorous, thought-provoking, real-life stories and practical ideas on how we can make our marriage everything we want it to be.

To accomplish that goal, we followed a style we started in our first two books, *"Daddy's Home"* (for men) and *Faithful Parents, Faithful Kids* (for parents): We went out and found the *real* experts. We talked to couples we've met over the years whom we respect and admire, and they also referred us to other husbands and wives who were enjoying *great* marriages in their second decade of love.

In all, we conducted long interviews with more than five

dozen couples. We heard their stories, we asked them to describe their secrets of success, and, basically, we wrung out good marriage ideas whenever we could. In most cases the names have been changed for confidentiality's sake.

We believe we've hit on many of the issues that couples struggle with during the second decade of love. It's our sincere hope that your investment in this book will propel your marriage to new levels of marital happiness. It's certainly done that for us!

The Stuff Nightmares
Are Made Of

every year between Christmas and the New Year, supermarket tabloids make the most outlandish predictions for the coming year. "Elvis Will Reappear as a Lounge Act in Peoria!" says one. "Hitler Will Be Discovered aboard a Submarine in the Bermuda Triangle!" screams another.

The hilarious headlines elicit some quiet chuckles as you wait for the lady in front of you to check out two carts of groceries. But what would happen if a reporter for *National Enquirer* was assigned to write some wild predictions about *your* future? What off-the-wall forecasts could he make about *your* marriage?

Joe and Suzy Christian's Marriage Defies the Experts!

Perhaps you've never given the matter much thought. But have you ever stopped and wondered what your married life will be like ten or twenty years from now? Yes, we know you're so busy that you can't even think about next week.

But we want you to take a moment and look into the not-too-distant future.

To help you get started, close your eyes, click your heels, and project yourself into this dream:

Your eyes slowly blink open in the dark room.

As you roll over, you check the red numbers illuminating the nightstand. It's 7:17 A.M. Another Saturday morning.

But this one is different: You're waking up with no children in the house. Besides a few days here and there, it's the first time that has happened in twenty-three years.

What makes this day even more unique is . . . they won't be back.

The nest is empty.

It's just you and your spouse.

Together.

Alone.

As you turn back over, you catch the sleeping silhouette of the person you said "I do" with so many years before. Time has passed quickly. Though some body parts have sagged and the hair has a slight silvery glint, it's the same person you used to dream about waking up with in those crazy courting days.

Your mind fast-forwards through footage of dozens of memories.

The kids were your life. Did you even have a life before kids?

Now they're gone, and it's just the two of you.

What are you thinking right now?

Does your marriage have you exchanging high fives . . . or is it a ho-hum affair?

Are you wondering if your relationship in coming years will be a rerun of the last five or ten?

Are you excited about the future, or are you plotting ways to do your own thing when the kids are gone?

While we hope most people reading these pages anticipate jumping for joy when the nest finally empties (with a twinge of sadness, of course), we're aware that many couples will be grieving. That first Saturday morning in an empty house could be a sad reminder that you're stuck in a marriage that didn't quite turn out like you'd planned. The spark in your relationship is past the point of a flicker.

> *Over the years, you made mistakes . . . but your spouse did, too. As you turn over once more in your warm bed, your eyes pop wide open.*
> *THIS ISN'T WHAT I EXPECTED MARRIAGE TO BE!*

Seasons Change

In the first years of marriage, it's just the two of you. Waking up with bad hair days and asking your spouse not to kiss you until you swished Listerine was fun! Remember?

Now you're in the child-rearing season of marriage. Your kids have filled your life with purpose and scores of Kodak moments. You finally understand what your parents did for *you*—and how God's plan for replenishing the next generation makes perfect sense.

But kids have also increased the pace of life. You're busy like never before: doctor visits, car pools, sports, music, and homework have run you down. You can't wait until the kids are in bed so you can enjoy twenty minutes of relaxation before hitting the sack—and starting all over in the morning.

Maybe you haven't had a meaningful conversation with your spouse in a week. But you both know that's to be expected because kids are high-maintenance items these days. *Oh, well, maybe we'll have some time together next week. . . .*

Looking ahead, the golden season of marriage begins the day the last child leaves for college. Our opening vignette asked a few questions about how you predict that day will be.

If you're afraid your mind will blare *THIS ISN'T WHAT I EXPECTED MARRIAGE TO BE!*—good! This is a healthy fear.

So what are you going to do about it?

Taking a few hours to read these pages is a start. We compiled our thoughts and ideas from dozens of couples in various seasons of marriage. Both of us are in the second decade of love, and we know firsthand the struggles couples like us are facing.

In addition, we are magazine editors at Focus on the Family and have access to reams of solid information.

With that thought in mind, here are four goals we want to share:

- to help you discover where your marriage is and how you got there;

- to show you that you're not alone when it comes to occasional feelings of disillusionment;

- to give you some hope and ideas on how to begin changing—if you want to;

♦ and to point you back to the person who made you one flesh with your mate. We will remind you that God's power and healing touch can resurrect even the weakest of marriages—and strengthen the strongest.

TOP TEN SIGNS THAT YOUR MARRIAGE MAY BE IN THE "DARK AGES"

10. Your most significant conversation in the past week had something to do with pizza toppings.

9. Your spouse gives you all the mail addressed to "occupant."

8. You think there's nothing wrong with your marriage.

7. The last time you went on a date, McDonald's had served only 4 trillion hamburgers.

6. You were watching your favorite sitcom and never noticed that your spouse left the room.

5. "What was that, dear?"

4. "Flowers? What are these for?"

3. Your Parcheesi game night was the most excitement you've had in months.

2. You insist that the wife call you "Sir."

1. When you see a couple kissing in public, your first word is *gross.*

A (Really) Brief History of Europe

Attention, class. Please open your history books to page 231. What? You weren't expecting a lesson on European history? Actually, we're going to take a little poetic license with three historical periods and relate them to modern-day marriage.

Do you remember the Middle Ages? They were also called the Dark Ages, and for good reason. That period in history—between A.D. 476 (the fall of the last Roman emperor) and 1453 (the fall of Constantinople to the Turks)—was slapped with the Dark Ages tag because much of Western Europe's classical civilization was over-run by barbarians. (Fortunately, religion also played a big role during those centuries. Historians often refer to the end of the Dark Ages as the Age of Faith. Later on, we'll be comparing the second season of love to the Age of Faith.)

Let's continue our history lesson. The Reformation began on October 31, 1517, when Martin Luther challenged the doctrines and practices of the Roman church by tacking his ninety-five theses on the Wittenberg door. Luther's intent was to reform the church from within. When that didn't occur, the northern Europe Lutheran movement eventually broke away and became Protestant.

Another important social and political movement at this time was called the *Renaissance,* a French term for *rebirth.* Historians have difficulty pinning a specific time to the beginning of this period, but they agree the Renaissance lasted until the middle of the seventeenth century.

The Renaissance was characterized by a revolt against the religious laws and worldliness of the Middle Ages. Scholars of the day concentrated on theology and ignored the classical heritage of Greece and Rome. Though this period brought on the rise of "humanism" (man being the measure of all things), it generally aroused western Europe from its lethargy, and it gave the people a new thirst for knowledge while placing a higher value on humans.

OK, Greg and Mike. How does all this relate to marriage?

The terms *Dark Ages, Reformation,* and *Renaissance* are handy in creating a word picture of where your relationship is, or where you want your relationship to be. Most marriages begin with lofty goals when couples have the time—and energy—to build their relationship brick by brick.

The onset of the parenting years, however, causes many couples to shift their focus and energy onto the kids. As we've said, nearly all parents derive a great amount of satisfaction during the twenty to thirty years of child rearing, even though the romantic side of marriage is often put on hold.

When the children are younger—and totally dependent upon the parents—marriages often go through what we call the "Dark Ages." No, not *everything* is dark. (Remember, kids bring incredible joy to a marriage.) But many couples aren't able to put much time into each other. Careers are advancing, homes are being furnished, and the kids are getting plugged into school, sports, and church activities.

These are *crucial* years for a couple. In fact, the median duration of all U.S. marriages that end in divorce is *seven* years. The reason: Like most, they began the marital years with a wrong or incomplete picture of marriage. From there they moved quickly into the Dark Ages, and before they knew what hit them, they were bailing out.

THE SEVEN-YEAR ITCH?

According to the U.S. National Center for Health Statistics, the average marriage lasts seven years before one or both of the spouses pull the plug. Here are the most recent statistics:

1970	6.7 years
1975	6.5 years
1980	6.8 years
1981	7.0 years
1982	7.0 years
1983	7.0 years
1984	6.9 years
1985	6.8 years
1986	6.9 years
1987	7.0 years
1988	7.1 year

How many children are usually involved? In the most recent survey taken in the late 1980s, 0.89 children were part and parcel of each divorce decree. That would be laughable except for the grim reminder that flesh and blood is involved. In addition, sons and daughters of divorced parents are rarely made "whole" in the intervening years.

Eventually, the husband or wife will notice that the relationship is heading into deep waters. (Our research shows that one person usually waits five to ten years before saying *anything*.)

This is the point where a relational Reformation needs to take place, or the Dark Ages will continue. Many couples, without a clue of how to make things right, can't see a way out of the parenting maze. The result? They live a marriage of convenience, or they divorce and find someone else.

When does this occur? Well, the first ten years of marriage are rough on a couple. But the second decade often makes or breaks a marriage.

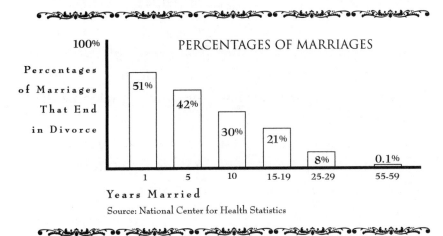

PERCENTAGES OF MARRIAGES

Percentages of Marriages That End in Divorce

100%

51%
42%
30%
21%
8%
0.1%

Years Married

1   5   10   15-19   25-29   55-59

Source: National Center for Health Statistics

If the couple can see through the thicket and agree a Reformation needs to take place—no matter how much work or pain is involved—their actions can lead to a Renaissance in their marriage. And it won't be a return to the honeymoon days before kids—it will be better!

A Strategy
Here are some crucial questions before we get started:

• Do you think you are still in the "Dark Ages" where the care of children or the pursuit of a career is valued above your marriage?

• Are you or your spouse ready for a change? Have you agreed that you want that change to occur together (instead of separately)?

+ Do you need some encouragement and ideas to help you move swiftly to a "Renaissance"?

We think it's possible to achieve that rebirth *before* the children leave home. Actually, you must! If the day comes when the kids are gone, and you wake up staring at someone you're not excited about spending the rest of your life with . . . you may not have the desire to rekindle the marriage flame.

That feeling is too awful to be described! Yet it's an *avoidable* tragedy—something we don't want to see happpen in our own marriages, nor in yours.

Which Renaissance Door Do You Want to Open?

Most men we talked to while researching this book admitted they thought a real Renaissance would be sex four times a week . . . like what many *said* they had in the first few years of marriage. (Well, maybe the first month.) After realizing how ridiculous that was, several pointed to the friendship they wished they could reestablish with their mate.

The Renaissance that women wanted wasn't too much different from what they expected when they walked down the aisle: a husband attentive to emotional needs, one who will talk, and one who will value her for who she is—not how well she cleans the house, cooks a casserole, or provides "services."

Before we talk about making a Renaissance happen in your marriage, let's take an overview of marriage in the 1990s. As you may have heard, if you've got a good marriage, you're in the minority.

What Model Have You Stuck With?

r ay and Sharon Gregory waited until their midtwenties before tying the knot. Ray hadn't been a Christian very long when he uttered his vows, but he looked forward to learning what it meant to become "one flesh" with his wife.

They settled in the Tampa Bay area, but the cost of living along Florida's Gold Coast was high. They managed to keep their "date night," even while on a tight budget, continued to work on communication, and slowly, yet deliberately, began moving toward the marriage they both had envisioned.

Their first daughter arrived three years after the wedding. Naturally, they showered her with the love first-time parents can give. Since they both wanted a large family, a son was born eighteen months later.

The joys of parenting were abundant, but a subtle shift was occurring. The two infants were taking up the bulk of Sharon's life. Although Ray was working hard for a local manufacturer, his world didn't revolve around his job. But

Sharon was different: She felt "needed" by her demanding children, and she was only too happy to throw herself at the kids. Sharon was raised in a home where alcohol was abused, so she was highly motivated to give her kids the happy childhood she never had. Her love, kisses, hugs, and attentiveness were all directed to them, not the big guy. Then their third child announced his arrival.

Ray knew he was being ignored, and he didn't like it. In a subconscious attempt to gain her attention, he blew his stack several times. He swore, raised his voice, and even pushed her around once or twice. This surprised and shocked Sharon. She had grown up around explosive tempers, and she thought she had put the past behind her. Though Ray always apologized profusely, he was losing Sharon's trust and respect—two ingredients necessary for an intimate marriage.

They agreed to see a counselor, who helped them unearth some deeply rooted issues in both of their lives. But Sharon still couldn't bring herself to forgive Ray. Her trust eroded because of his outbursts, and their sex life went to near zero. For months at a time, she never made herself available.

"I love my wife and family, but our marriage is headed nowhere," said Ray. "Since I'm a committed Christian, I know what God says about divorce, seeking other women, or viewing pornography. I'm stuck."

How does he handle it?

"For the past two years, I've come home each day with a happy face, and really try to live my life as unto the Lord. That helps *my* attitude, but there's not much progress between Sharon and me. She puts her time into the kids, does the domestic thing, but she seems to have no interest in me or the marriage."

Both will admit that after only nine years, their relationship has evolved into a marriage of convenience. While counseling continues to uncover hidden problems, they're not totally out of the woods.

The Seven Models of Marriage

In one of my (Greg's) interviews, I spoke with Jan David Hettinga, a veteran pastor living in Bothell, Washington. He's counseled hundreds of couples in his twenty-five years of ministry, and over that span he has observed that most marriages can fit into one of seven different categories. The first six, he admits, comprise more than 80 percent of the couples in the church.

Jan's given us permission to share these seven models of marriage with you. Our goal isn't to explain *every* box that a marriage can be put in, but to point you toward the model for a Renaissance marriage.

1. Male Dominant, Female Compliant

Because of his insecurity, a poor fatherly example, or an inaccurate biblical view of the husband's role, the man feels obligated to run roughshod over his wife. He makes all the decisions, and his wife is anything but a fellow heir in Christ. For whatever reasons, the wife is too weak to challenge her husband's "authority." On the rare occasions she stands up to him she's met with a torrent of verbal—or physical—abuse. She learns it's better to stay in the background.

2. Female Dominant, Male Compliant

These types of relationships don't happen by accident.

Somewhere along the line, the woman has learned to be ultra-self-reliant—to a fault. She may have grown up in a home where her mother walked all over her dad; thus, she views men as weak. Later on, she gravitated toward men she could control. Guess what? She hooked one.

Likewise, the man could have had a weak father and a domineering mother. He craved his mother's love; therefore, he unconsciously sought out a woman just like her. His father exemplified no real strength, so like his wife, he simply follows the pattern set at home.

3. Two Equally Dominant People, Verbally Duking It Out

When two strong wills collide, watch the fireworks fly! The marriage settles into trench warfare, with each side lobbing hand grenades. Who will prevail?

4. "We Fight, But He Wins"

The couple fights for dominance, but the man always wins. To stay on top, his taunts become dirtier and nastier. Consequently, she always gives in to keep peace and shield the kids from his influence.

5. "We Fight, But She Wins"

The man will resist for a while, but he eventually concludes the conflict isn't worth it, so he throws in the towel. Besides, if he puts up too good a fight, she'll deny him sex. That's too high a cost.

6. Separate Lives Together

Like Ray and Sharon, the couple we met a few pages ago, the

marriage has regressed into an "arrangement." *You go your way, I'll go mine. Maybe we'll meet each other's emotional and sexual needs, maybe we won't.* Though one person often controls this arrangement, it's usually by mutual agreement. The husband reasons: *The wife has the kids; I have my job and hobbies. We don't believe in divorce [yet], so we'll tolerate the inattention to each other and find other ways to fill the void.*

That line of thinking, says Pastor Hettinga, is the model for many contemporary marriages—including Christian couples. It's a recipe for disaster, not just for the husband and wife, but also for the children who grow up in such an environment.

Where Do You Fit?

Nearly all of the couples we interviewed fit into one of these six models at one time or another. Perhaps you saw your marriage in one of those categories, too. If so, that's exactly where Satan wants you and your spouse because he *hates* marital oneness. Unless there is a Reformation, your marriage will stay mired in the Dark Ages.

By now, you're probably wondering what the seventh marriage model is, the one Jan said 20 percent of Christian couples actually attain. It is the Renaissance we want to point you toward.

7. Mutual Submission to Jesus Christ

These couples have laid aside their power struggles and surrendered to Christ their desire—and it's a *real* desire—to control the other person. By choosing mutually to submit, they're granted the grace and strength to overcome their problems.

This is the biblical model for marriage that all of us have

heard so much about from Ephesians 5:22-28. In case it's been awhile since you've read that passage, here it is:

> *Wives, submit to your husbands as to the Lord. For the husband is the head of the wife as Christ is the head of the church, his body, of which he is the Savior. Now as the church submits to Christ, so also wives should submit to their husbands in everything.*
>
> *Husbands, love your wives, just as Christ loved the church and gave himself up for her to make her holy, cleansing her by the washing with water through the word, and to present her to himself as a radiant church, without stain or wrinkle or any other blemish, but holy and blameless. In this same way, husbands ought to love their wives as their own bodies. He who loves his wife loves himself.*

What's Ahead?

A worthy goal, isn't it? To help you get there—and ourselves, too (because we're also in the middle of this second decade thing)—we'll be relating stories from couples smack in the middle of the Dark Ages, those who are making a Reformation, and those who are enjoying a Renaissance.

We've already brushed by the primary reason why marriages in the second decade of love are stuck in the Dark Ages: the time pressures that naturally occur when children arrive. Our next chapter will describe why couples struggle during these child-rearing years and how some couples found their way through this time of "darkness."

3

And Baby Makes Three
(or Four, or Five)

*P*arents don't have very long memories. When we asked couples what life was like B.C. (Before Children), we often heard this response: "I dunno."

Who *can* imagine life without that towheaded blond learning his *ABCs* or the artistic daughter who loves to finger-paint the dining room walls? Besides, any of the difficulties we experienced bringing a child into this world—the bouts of infertility, the long, nineteen-hour labor, the painful sitz baths—vanished moments after we held that little one in our arms.

But if the courtship, wedding, and honeymoon represent a storybook beginning to marriage, the screams of a wife delivering her first child are enough to jolt any couple.

A New Way of Thinking
Yes, the couples we talked with said having children changed their marriage relationship. *(That, and husbands leaving their*

dirty socks on the floor.) But as couples gravitated to new roles, how did their marriage change? Were mothers who poured themselves into the kids—often at the same time fathers were working long hours to climb the career ladder—mindful of the dwindling contact with their spouse?

Often, in the excitement of becoming parents, couples fail to notice their gaze has quickly turned from each other to that cute little bugger. They'll do *anything* for him in those heady first few months. But time zips by, and Junior is soon big enough to rock his Johnny Jump Up and scrape hallway walls with his walker. Life settles into a routine, but that routine often doesn't include building up the marriage relationship. Here's a typical story:

"We waited five years before having kids," said Kerry Jackson. "We enjoyed every minute of a nice, long honeymoon. But it was a pretty rude awakening when the children came along. My husband and I had to adapt, and that took some doing. We were both schoolteachers used to living independent lives. When our first child arrived, we socially faded away. We stayed at home because we didn't have any grandparents nearby, and we weren't real confident with baby-sitters."

Right around the eight-year mark, the Jacksons' marriage hit the Dark Ages. A second child was born, and Kerry felt like the world was closing in on her. The kids were a handful, and she didn't think she was doing a good job with the discipline problems that cropped up. Although she and her husband, Trent, were raised in the church, they had stopped attending weekly services.

"That was the shakiest time in our marriage," said Kerry.

"We were not being grounded in God's Word, and it seemed as though we were going through life without a foundation. Too much trial and error was happening."

Trent and Kerry failed to use any of their limited spare time to carry on a coherent conversation; they figured it just wasn't in the cards. "We did not do anything together because everything was centered around the kids," said Kerry. "Our relationship suffered from neglect, and I began to feel he didn't love me anymore. Trent never was affectionate to begin with, but then he had a hard time kissing me every day, or giving me little hugs. He pulled back because he thought I didn't want any affection since I was so busy with the kids."

That last sentence is a telling one. Because Trent's wife was *so* involved with feedings, diapers, and baths, he shrugged his shoulders and figured he wasn't part of the program. But he was.

Like Trent, I (Mike) carried the same feelings, too, when our children, Andrea and Patrick, were infants. My wife, Nicole, is so competent, so hardworking with the kids that I'd come home from work to a tornado of activity. I figured it would be best to remain in the shadows. *If I stay out of her way, she'll cope better,* I thought.

Our physical contact dwindled. I'd wave good-bye in the morning and step out of her life. Then I'd come home and have trouble fitting into the "get-them-fed, get-them-bathed, and get-them-into-bed-before-I-drop-from-exhaustion" phase. Sure, I pitched in, but Nicole and I were so busy we didn't have time to make eye contact. Once the kids were down and we caught our breath, it was *our* bedtime.

I can't remember the exact occasion, but Nicole took the lead one morning as I rushed to get out the door for work. (Guys aren't good at this stuff, but that's a poor excuse.)

"Aren't you going to kiss me before you leave?" she asked.

"Why should I?" I said teasingly.

No sooner were the words out of my mouth than I knew I should be laying a lip lock on Nicole. That became the genesis of a hard-and-fast rule in our house. These days, before I leave for work, I give Nicole a good-morning kiss. When I arrive home, I welcome her with another, and when the lights go out, we pucker up again. After ten years of smooching, it feels funny *not* to kiss at these junctures of the day.

But back to the Jacksons. How were they able to move from the Dark Ages toward a Renaissance? First, they had a Reformation.

"We started going to church again," said Kerry. "Once we started doing that, we realized how much we were trying to do on our own. We were not looking toward God to lead us.

"We learned we had to stay in touch with God *and* Christian friends. We got into a fellowship group at church where every other week we met with several other couples for a Bible study. It became like family for us. I can look back now and see we were not in contact with a lot of people. We could feel that, and we knew we were stagnating. You can't grow if you're only in the Word, but don't spend time with other Christians. My advice to young couples is to make time to meet with other Christian couples so you can share your child-raising concerns and problems. They *will* help you grow."

TOP TEN REASONS WHY THE WIFE MAY PREFER SPENDING TIME WITH THE KIDS THAN WITH YOU

10. The kids make comments about her cooking—even if they're all negative ones.

9. They sometimes act like they're actually happy to see her when they get home.

8. You still think she's joking when she complains about your breath.

7. The kids don't sleep when they watch TV.

6. The kids don't watch TV when they sleep.

5. The kids don't know how to use the remote control yet.

4. They're learning to speak in complete sentences.

3. They can hug and kiss without expecting you know what.

2. The kids actually talk to her.

1. The kids have seen the *Oprah* shows she most wants to discuss.

What We Learned

For the Jacksons, getting back into fellowship with other believers was the first step. But their twice-a-month Bible studies were the only time they went out together. Though that's a start, our advice to couples of young children is do *everything you can* to get out of the house—without kids—a few times a month, be it to a Bible study, a coffee shop, or a bowling alley. Remember, you *need* this time together since the potential for your marriage to head into the Dark Ages is at its greatest. (We'll have more on communication and dating ideas in chapter 5.)

One Size Fits All?

A question for Mom: Did you walk away from a flourishing career after the birth of your firstborn? How did that affect your self-esteem? Were you the only stay-at-home mom on the block? We understand (since both our wives are stay-at-home moms) that you're underappreciated by society—and sometimes by your husband, too.

A question to another mom: Are you working outside the home in addition to being a mother? Has it been hard finding suitable day care? Does it feel as though you never sleep enough to "catch up"?

Parenthood comes in different forms these days, and there's no one-size-fits-all advice. That's why we will take a broad approach for the rest of this chapter. If you're in your early years of parenthood, reach for a highlighter. Or, if you're an experienced parent, it's OK to nod your head as we go along. Look for yourself and your spouse in the following stories.

Career or Mommy Track?

When Amy McDonald was twenty-three years old, she was close to earning a teaching credential. She wasn't about to let marriage or a kid mess up her career plans.

Then Amy fell in love with Chuck, and some of the hard-edged corners rounded off. *OK,* she thought. *I'll get married, but Chuck better not expect me to have any rug rats running around.*

After the McDonalds had been married four years, Chuck sat her down after church one Sunday afternoon.

"I think we should seriously start thinking about having children," Chuck said.

"But I'm only twenty-seven," she replied. "What's the big rush? Besides, you know how I feel about kids."

A month later, Chuck had a twinkle in his eye. "Very soon, God has a blessing for you," he whispered in her ear.

That seemed strange. But she *did* become pregnant, and Amy was not a happy camper. "I cried a lot those nine months, and they had to lead me to the delivery room kicking and screaming. But I left the hospital with a whole new perspective after I held that newborn in my arms," said Amy.

"Looking back, I wish someone had told me that having children is really neat, because I had always thought that I needed a career, but it turned out that wasn't the case at all. I'm doing the most important thing anyone could do— helping shape another's life and seeing common events through the eyes of a child."

What We Learned

A husbands needs to be mindful of his wife's feelings *before* and *after* the kids arrive. Amy was a bonafide baby boomer, growing up in an era—the late sixties and early seventies— that exalted individuality. She, along with millions of other young women, was told by society that she could "have it all"—marriage, career, and kids. But after giving birth, Amy knew for her that was a hollow slogan.

Young mothers who try to burn the candle at both ends— combining career and kids—have it tough. Amy was one of those who discovered it was better to jump off the career path and try the "Mommy Track" for a while. Husbands should support their wives when they make this difficult decision, and young mothers should remind themselves that they need to do what's *best* for their *children.*

Sudden Impact

How many couples with young children realize they are traveling through the fast-moving river of child raising? When your family boat is bouncing up and down in a section of the rapids, are you thinking, *I sure hope we make it?* Parents should be looking for opportunities to paddle over to the shoreline for some R and R.

Getting married was so natural, so convenient for Jeff and Louise Mayer that they had no clue a little kid would put them on that raging river.

"Before our first boy came along, Louise and I loved being spontaneous. We enjoyed walking together on warm Texas evenings, because that was something we started when we got engaged," said Jeff.

With Caleb reigning from the high chair, however, the Mayers' focus shifted from each other to the new star of the show. Just going to the local supermarket meant logistical planning on the order of the Normandy invasion. The Mayers had to load the car with diaper bags, extra clothes, an umbrella, bottles with juice, and prepared formula. When their second son was born a couple of years later, their workload increased exponentially. Caring for two infants exhausted Louise, and Jeff—bushed from a long workday—tried to help out when he arrived home.

Dinner was another experience altogether. Louise would begin to say something to Jeff when Caleb would flip a spoonful of applesauce at his younger brother.

Oops! Dinner was finished. Time to launch into the kids' nightly routine: bath, brush teeth, Bible story, and get them to bed. No wonder the couple's communication shriveled up like a desert flower in June.

"The challenges to our relationship became more intense," says Jeff. "When we did get a chance to talk, it seems all we chatted about was family business. She'd say, 'This happened at the market today,' or 'So-and-so dropped by'—factual kind of information. Since I'm at work all day, I've had my fill of adult conversation—but she hadn't. Louise wanted to sit around and talk on a more emotional level with me, yet with kids on the scene, I forgot how to do that. When we went to bed each evening, she wanted to stay up and talk. I didn't. I was tired and wanted to sleep."

What We Learned

Time and time again, couples coming out of the Dark Ages told us two things: (1) Don't delay (for very long) talking about something that's bugging you; and (2) late nights, when both parents are pooped, are not the best times for deep conversation. "Talk before ten" was the advice we heard.

Handicapped Child, Handicapped Marriage?

We had many parents tell us they entered the parenting phase with a certain amount of fear because of their own childhoods. "I was afraid to have kids," said Sally Samuels. "I had been raised in a perfectionistic home, and I went through a lot of emotional abuse—and I don't use those words lightly. My husband, Bill, and I really prayed, 'Lord, please give us an easy child, and make it a boy.' I felt that if I had a daughter, I would be more likely to repeat the perfectionism scenario."

Sally's first child, Nathan, was a breeze, but Seth was born three years later with ataxia—a condition in which the brain doesn't grow. He was also born deaf. Each day Sally wondered what new ailment would manifest itself. It often seemed that all Seth saw the first four years of life was his car seat or a doctor's waiting room. "We had *so* many doctor's appointments," Sally says, "that we went to five or ten office visits a week. I assumed everything was wrong with Seth until the doctor said something was right."

Sally wasn't looking for pity when we talked to her. "No one ever stands at the altar and thinks they are going to have a handicapped child some day, but I would never trade Seth for another child. He is my son, and I love him dearly. But the stress of handling him is so hard, especially because he is also hyperactive. It's like having a lion in the house. Every time I turn around, something is falling off the shelves. While I'm cleaning up mess number one, he's making mess number two."

Every couple of weeks, Sally will say to her husband, "I need a date." She's fed up with hearing, "I have to go potty" all day. Sally desires adult conversation. "It's so nice to go out to a restaurant, and when your food comes out, you don't have to cut it up in little pieces."

The Samuelses say they need to date twice a month (the bare minimum, we would say) to make time for their marriage. On the plus side, they do weekend getaways twice a year. "Otherwise, your kids become all-consuming," explained Sally. "You have to make time in your marriage for each other. The way we do it is by networking with other parents of handicapped children. We'll watch their kids for a weekend in exchange for leaving our two boys with them. That has been a real blessing, because we've reached points where we couldn't do it anymore; we had to get away by ourselves. Having those long weekends together keeps us going."

What We Learned

A handicapped child puts stresses on a marriage like few things can. We can't even pretend to understand the twenty-four-hour commitment it takes. Networking with other families and trading off baby-sitting duties was a smart move.

When Sally told Bill she needed a date, he stepped into action. That's the sign of a couple who's going to enjoy the hectic second decade of love, despite the curveball that was thrown at them.

Getting Off the Dark Age Track

If you're past the early years when those wonderful bundles of joy inadvertently slid your relationship into the Dark Ages, then these stories may have simply been a reminder of the ghost of marriage past.

Sadly, however, most couples moved blindly from the early child-rearing years, when children monopolized the airspace at home, to several more years of the Dark Ages.

Why? It was certainly not intentional, but they blithely continued down the marital road in the same gear—without pulling into a rest stop.

Romance can't happen on the fly; it needs to percolate, build up some steam, and reach a crescendo before starting the cycle all over again. Those who try to short-circuit the process—a husband who demands that his sexual needs be met pronto, a battle-fatigued wife who "checks out" of the relationship emotionally—will remain in the Dark Ages.

That's why we are so big on taking time away from the kids on a periodic basis. Couples who find the time to snatch an evening out or make long-range plans for a three-day weekend together will have a better chance of maintaining some semblance of balance between kids and marriage. We hope we made our point.

The stories in this chapter illustrate an all-too-common trend for parents who allow their marriage to go on cruise control when baby makes three. It can be marriage-threatening to stay on it too long; you may fall asleep at the wheel.

Children weren't the only pothole on the tollway to a marital Renaissance. Emotional baggage, poor role models, dysfunctional families—call it what you want—but your childhood shaped who you are, how you parent, and how you relate to your spouse. We found that out . . . BIG-TIME!

The Great American
(Dysfunctional) Family

i (Mike) will admit the dark truth: I grew up in a normal home. While Dad pounded nails in the hot sun at the construction site, Mom never worked outside the home a day in her life. While she was a volunteer playground monitor at school, Dad juggled his work schedule so he could coach my Little League baseball teams. They're the only parents I've ever known in my forty years on this earth.

Boy, I sure had a weird upbringing, didn't I?

Seriously, I realize how fortunate I am to have been raised in a stable setting—especially after Greg and I finished researching this book! Time and again in our interviews, we heard tales of emotional abuse, off-the-wall role models, and parents who couldn't stay away from the bottle. Here's a quick sampling:

- From a thirty-five-year-old father: "Dad never showed any affection. It's hard for me to give affection; I just wanted to get it. Being raised that way makes it hard to change later on."

- From a forty-eight-year-old woman: "My mom was an only child, but Dad was a rebel when he married her. He was self-centered and had a chip on his shoulder. They played a lot of emotional games. There were a lot of meals I couldn't finish because I was crying."

- From a thirty-three-year-old woman: "My father was an alcoholic; my mother abandoned us for six years. My advice to couples: Try to get healing *before* you get married."

- From a fifty-two-year-old man: "I was thirty-eight when I heard my mother say 'I love you' for the first time. I was taught not to hurt or feel growing up. We were so mechanical."

- From a thirty-seven-year-old woman: "My mom subtly taught me to be flirtatious and seductive. I have a hard time relating to men without thinking sexually."

The sorry state of many modern marriages can be traced back to the midsixties, when society's foundations shook and nearly toppled. *Time* magazine asked, "Is God Dead?" on its cover in April of 1966, and many answered yes. The narcissistic me-decade of the seventies wasn't much better, either. Those were tumultuous times for anyone growing up—and hard on parents, too. *Everyone's* values were rocked by the sea of change in social mores.

Divorce laws were liberalized in the late sixties, which made it easier for husbands to trade in the old lady for a newer, trimmer model. On the flip side, no-fault divorce opened the door for wives to dump their deadbeat husbands. And what about the children? *Hey, kids are resilient. They'll bounce back.*

That was the prevailing wisdom back then, but the results of two decades of social upheaval are in, and while Dad and Mom may have found personal fulfillment after the split, the kids often became damaged goods.

One of the most remarkable articles in recent years appeared in the April 1993 *Atlantic Monthly*. Titled "Dan Quayle Was Right," author Barbara Dafoe Whitehead skewered the liberal dogma that variations of the intact, two-parent family—single moms and stepfamilies—don't undermine society.

> *Contrary to popular belief, many children do not "bounce back" after divorce or remarriage. Difficulties that are associated with family breakup often persist into adulthood. Children who grow up in single-parent or steparent families are less successful as adults, particularly in the two domains of life—love and work—that are most essential to happiness. Needless to say, not all children experience such negative effects. However, research shows that many children from disrupted families have a harder time* achieving intimacy in a relationship, forming a stable marriage, *or even holding a steady job* [emphasis added].

Now we're in the 1990s, with the last wave of baby boomers sailing through their thirties. Many are in the midst of the first decade of marriage when problems crop up. In a knee-jerk fashion, young couples sometimes revert to behavior they saw growing up—an abusive father who lashes out at a timid wife, the mom who drinks wine coolers all afternoon while parked in front of TV soaps, or the dad who blows the budget playing the state lottery.

Some young people married spouses with built-in problems of their own, thus beginning a new cycle of "codependency" (a relationship where you are "dependent" on one another to fuel each other's sickness).

It's amazing how people with codependent personalities can find each other. Have you ever wondered how a young, innocent waif falls in love with a brooding, abusive guy? It's probably because she grew up in a home where her father was emotionally absent. Perhaps she even saw him abuse her mother. She continues that pattern because that's the only world she knows—and feels comfortable with. Also, she unconsciously may be trying to heal her relationship with her father by making *this* one work. We're not psychologists, but you hear about this stuff all the time.

Getting Personal

What about the family background that puts *your* marriage together? Did your parents divorce? Were either of you raised by a stepparent? Did Mom and Dad barely speak to each other—and then yell to make their point? Was there some sort of verbal, emotional, physical, or sexual abuse? If so, this chapter should help you recognize some of the "baggage" you may have brought to your marriage, and we'll look at ways you can treat your spouse *if* his or her dysfunctional family background crops up.

Obviously, we can't detail *every* form of dysfunction. We'll leave that to books by trained professionals. The taste we offer, however, should be enough to allow you to discern whether your own background is keeping your marriage in the Dark Ages. If you think it is, we offer a ray of hope—it doesn't have to stay that way! With Jesus Christ at the center of the marriage, dozens of the individuals we spoke with overcame terrible backgrounds and have happy, successful marriages today.

Wide-open Marriage

When Emilie Beach came of age in the 1960s, her parents were urbane intellectuals who could have stepped out of the pages of a Jean-Paul Sartre novel. Emilie's parents had an "open marriage," which meant that each side tolerated the other's affairs. Although this arrangement had been in place since the day she was born, Emilie didn't catch on until she was sixteen.

On Saturday nights, for instance, Mom would dress up, style her hair, and apply the right shade of rouge to her cheeks. Dad, who drew baby-sitting duty that night, would comment how pretty she looked. They'd kiss in the doorway and wish each other well. "I'm going dancing," Emilie would hear her mom say. Then she was off into the night—and into the arms of another man.

Emilie's grandparents also had an open marriage, so it wasn't hard for her parents to fall into a "don't ask, don't tell" state of matrimony. A divorce would only complicate matters for the kids, they agreed, so it was better to stay together while they pursued their own happiness without the encumbrances of fidelity.

How enlightened.

Emilie wasn't being ushered to Sunday school every week (her parents obviously were not churchgoers), but something in her heart told her this wasn't the best plan for marriage. She would watch "Father Knows Best" on reruns and fantasize that actor Robert Young was her dad. "I wanted to be raised in a traditional home so badly," she said.

When she was in her early twenties, Emilie became a Christian—and met an earnest young man named Paul. He, too, had grown up in a nontraditional family. His parents divorced when he was four, sending his mom back into the work force. She married her boss when Paul turned eleven, the same year his natural father died. His stepfather was a loving person and a good role model for the young lad. It wasn't hard for Paul to call him "Dad."

When Paul and Emilie fell in love, she shared her parents' past with Paul, who nodded and said fine. But her background was a ticking time bomb, and when trials came during the Dark Ages, their marriage nearly blew up.

First of all, Paul was still attending a state university when they married. "That drove me nuts," said Emilie, who is four years older than Paul. "I had already done the 'poor-and-in-college' bit. I wanted to have some money. I wanted to be able to afford more than Campbell's tomato soup."

Paul noticed another thing: She could not compromise. She had to have her own way.

"I fought marriage tooth and nail," said Emilie. "I wanted to be a free, independent woman, free to do what I wanted, when I pleased. I even took vacations on my own. I can remember going all alone to a dude ranch for a week after we had been married four years. I wanted to be this free-spirited person who could never be put in a mold."

Her two older sisters egged her on. "This is the sister who does what she wants," one bragged to friends. A tall California blonde with cheerleader looks, Emilie loved to drive her convertible and let the wind blow in her hair.

Although one side of Paul admired her independence, he ached to be "one" with her. They couldn't agree on anything. If he said they were driving north, she would argue that they were heading west. Their knockdown, drag-out fights became legendary with their friends, who shook their heads when they witnessed the intensity of their verbal battles. Somehow, the young couple always found it within themselves to make up.

Even so, Emilie, older and more worldly, didn't respect Paul very much. After two years, she wanted a separation. "Our marriage isn't working," she announced.

Here's where Paul used his head. Using a *Love Must Be Tough* strategy, he told Emilie that they would either make the marriage work or they would divorce. But there would be no trial separation.

"I'm not going into limbo," he said. *Besides, with your background, you'll probably have an affair if we separate,* he thought.

"OK," she replied, "let's get some counseling."

And so off they went to a Social Services counselor, where the fee was based on their ability to pay. "It wasn't the best counseling, but we learned to listen to each other and take some responsibility," said Paul. "Until we realized those things, we were reacting to each other, instead of listening."

What We Learned

Although they were Christians, Paul and Emilie didn't have much to fall back on when the marriage went south. Paul's instinctive reaction that a separation would doom the marriage was correct. Admitting that they needed counseling forced them to face their problems head-on. They learned that marriage was not an I'll-do-my-thing-until-we-see-each-other-next-time proposition. Today, the Beaches have been married ten years, and their relationship has never been better. They are looking forward to the second decade of love.

Purple Haze

When we asked Gail O'Sullivan to state one positive thing about her parents' marriage, she drew a blank. But then again, her parents abused alcohol—a lot. Gail's mom, a school secretary, usually began her daily binge with a couple of noontime highballs at a nearby restaurant. When her father arrived home from work at five o'clock, he shook a pitcher of martinis at the wet bar. Then it was off to the easy chair, where he replenished his empty glass until he slumped off to bed.

Gail grew up believing marriage was an institution of maintaining equilibrium. Since her parents were in an alcoholic stupor most of the time, the marriage did not grow. They supported each other's habit, and the only time her parents pulled from the same string was when they had to stand up to Gail or one of her brothers.

"I can remember Mom talking about my oldest brother, who is very successful in the world's view," said Gail. "He got a divorce the year before I got married. What I heard over and over from my mom was this: Since my never-do-wrong brother couldn't maintain a marriage, I had no chance."

Gail became a Christian just before she met Eric. Although she knew she didn't have much to go on, Gail read everything she could get her hands on about marriage. She interviewed older couples from their church and asked them how they worked through conflict. She memorized the ingredients of good communication. Despite her efforts to shore up her end, Gail married a young man who was raised by his father after his mom left the marriage. To save himself from emotional pain, Eric had a tendency to flee difficult situations.

The day after their first child, Whitney, was born, Eric signed up for a citywide tennis tournament. Meanwhile, at the hospital, a painfully sore Gail attended all the new baby and parenting classes. Not Eric. He made an "appearance" between matches.

"I was doing a slow burn," said Gail. "I assumed he was avoiding me because of a lack of love. Why else would he do it? When he finally came to the hospital, I told him his actions were killing me. He shrugged his shoulders and looked at the floor. His reply was, 'I gotta go. I have a match in fifteen minutes.' Having an escape protected him from conflict."

What We Learned

The O'Sullivans had been caught in choppy waters, but they looked to Christ to keep their boat upright. We can report some progress, but Eric still has trouble attaching himself to someone he loves. Growing up without a mother, he never learned how he should relate to a woman. The O'Sullivans still have a ways to go, and in the meantime, Eric needs to pick up the slack by reading marriage books, watching Gary Smalley and John Trent videos, and seeking out mentors. Gail, however, may need to nudge him toward those resources because of Eric's dysfunctional background. (We'll be talking more about that subject in our next chapter.)

He's Not There

Penny Sims wishes she had known more about adult children of alcoholics before saying "I do"—because she married one. Right around her eighth anniversary, she was bewildered: Every time she tried to engage her husband, Richard, he was not there emotionally.

"I assumed I was stuck with this marriage—one where my husband was smiling, friendly, but distant," said Penny. The home life had fallen into a predictable pattern. Whenever she asked Richard an open-ended question, he would mumble an answer that never addressed the issue. When she pressed him, he got up and said he had to work in the garden or the garage.

One evening, Penny shook a test tube filled with urine. "Hey Richard, I'm pregnant," she yelled from the bathroom. "Can you believe it? I guess the birth control failed."

"That's nice," came the reply from the living room.

"Well, what do you think about having a second child?"

"I don't know. Do you want to have an abortion?"

"Do I want a what? Richard, we're Christians. You know abortion is not an option."

"Oh, I guess you're right."

That was Penny's first inkling something was amiss—that Richard was not emotionally involved. Another thing she noticed was that he could never buy her a nice, romantic gift. He would go Christmas shopping and return empty-handed; ditto for her birthday.

"I thought that was odd," said Penny. "But in order to buy a gift, he would have to follow through with an emotional commitment. His father never could buy gifts, either. At Christmastime, he would walk around and hand everyone fifty dollars. That's a very cold way of giving Christmas gifts."

Right about this time, their five-year-old daughter, Tawna, was having temper tantrums. She was a *strong*-willed child. The situation deteriorated so much that they decided to seek counseling. At the first session, the counselor asked Richard several neutral questions to describe himself.

After listening a few moments, the counselor announced, "You are an adult child of an alcoholic."

Richard blanched.

"Yes, that's true," he said.

Richard hadn't revealed his family background to Penny prior to marriage. The question never came up in their premarital counseling. *By the way, Richard, are either of your parents drunks?*

After that news was set on the table, Penny understood why their marriage lacked intimacy or those touches that say *I care*: gifts for Mother's Day, flowers before a three-day weekend, a candlelight dinner for two.

The counselor began dredging up the past. She learned

that Richard's father was a career Navy man. His sea tours lasted six, eight, even twelve months at a time, especially during the Vietnam War.

When his father was home, he liked to keep a buzz on. Sooner or later the alcohol intake produced an explosion— and the family would duck for cover. The kids kept their distance. One way they survived was to make themselves emotionally unavailable: "Please pass the gravy" was the extent of their dinner conversation. They also learned how to present themselves as a "good family" in front of company.

When Richard told the counselor that he had never received a personal gift from his father, the therapist suggested this idea: Since it was Christmastime (and near their wedding anniversary date of December 18), she asked Richard to buy Penny a small gift every day leading up to Christmas.

"Believe it or not, Richard came up with seven romantic gifts," said Penny. "He started with a pretty sweater, something a younger person would wear, and he said he was giving this to someone who was still young at heart. Then he gave me a glass vase for all the times he didn't bring home roses. Next, he presented me with a Christmas ornament in the shape of a heart. He purchased another ornament with a bear and Goldilocks. And finally, he found a set of pretty dishes on sale. Really incredible. Not having to come up with one blockbuster present was very freeing to him."

Now Richard *looks* for ways to be romantic. Recently, he had to come up with a four-digit number to access his voice mail at work. He picked his wedding anniversary date: 12-18.

"A little thing like that sends a signal to me," said Penny. "The message is this: Richard is madly in love—with me! But to spend the first eight years not knowing how this guy *really* felt about me was very difficult. Today, our marriage has never been better."

What We Learned
Couples can hide a dysfunctional past for a while, but sooner or later, living together peels away all the layers. Richard and Penny were drifting apart during the Dark Ages, and his type of unavailability sinks many marriages. Fortunately, a counselor helped him recall his difficult past, and the couple was able to rebuild.

Looking to Other Areas

Kathie Cranbee says she has a sunny personality because she was raised in a good family where love was passed around. Her husband, Brian, however, grew up in the shadow of a difficult father who verbally abused him every step of the way.

Brian and Kathie were so madly in love that they thought it would conquer everything. Brian was excited. He'd finally found someone who loved him unconditionally.

The first few years of married life went well, but then the Dark Ages hit. Right around their seventh anniversary, Kathie miscarried twice, which plunged her into deep grief. Brian submerged his pain because Kathie was so open about hers.

"I had a real crisis of faith," said Kathie. "I was angry at God. I didn't understand why he would allow two miscarriages to happen. At the same time, Brian was in his first pastorate, and he was well liked. Right away, however, he had to deal with some severe crises in the church family, and it seemed he took on the burdens of those he was counseling. When he added our personal problems to the heap, he fell into a bout of deep depression. Me? I was just mad at God."

With their relationship on hold, they wondered what life would throw them next. The stress reached a point where they didn't know if the marriage was worth saving. "We both got help, and we were able to put the pieces back together," said Kathie. "We didn't have a clue what was happening; that's how messed up we were. I asked a friend for a name of a counselor, and we both went in and did some one-on-one therapy. While I stayed home, Brian went to Kentucky for some heavy-duty counseling to deal with his depression. He used his time to pray, reflect, and study God's Word.

"I can remember when he came home, and he treated me differently. He tried to win me back again. He sent a rose to me at work. Written on the card was a message from the song 'The Rose,' sung by Bette Midler. It said: 'In the winter, beneath the bitter snow, lies the seed that with the sun's love in the spring becomes the rose.'"

What We Learned

Many couples think everything is going to turn out fine when they leave that bad family behind. Love can conquer a lot, but only Christ can conquer everything. Our conversations convinced us that Christ . . . plus a trained Christian counselor . . . were often necessary to overcome the high hurdles of a dysfunctional past.

Since you may be close to—or in the middle of—the second decade of love, you can probably point to behaviors in your spouse that show that the way he or she was raised was anything but healthy.

If you're not sure what signs to look for, here are a few of the main ones:

- Disappearing acts during family events (holidays, reunions, and birthdays)

- An unwillingness (and sometimes an inability) to talk about feelings when it seems the situation calls for some sort of response

- Extreme and/or frequent outbursts of anger or aggressive behavior

- Frequent bouts of depression, especially if it's the debilitating variety

- Lack of desire to socialize or become better friends with peers

- Obvious avoidance of contact with a parent or relative

- Abuse of alcohol or drugs

- Inability to stop other addictions, including gambling, pornography, lying, and stealing

HELPING A HURTING SPOUSE

- Pray that memories and strongholds in a spouse's life would be supernaturally tended to by the Great Physician. Jesus Christ is the ultimate source of power and protection from a past shaped by the sins of others.

- If the offending spouse treats you or the family poorly, he or she still needs to take ownership of the behavior. Until that happens, he or she will simply blame others for the problems. All this communicates is that the spouse doesn't want to change. Understanding the problem and relaying unconditional love is important, but the greater love points him or her toward long-term solutions (usually counseling).

- If a spouse's behavior is affecting you or the children and you don't know what to do about it, it's time to seek outside help. A pastor or other trained health professionals are your best source. If, however, the counseling therapy doesn't include a belief that we are each accountable for our sins, the treatment will not go deep enough. The latest in pop psychology cannot reach the root cause of poor behavior.

- Never use the behavior of a hurting spouse as a weapon to hurt or manipulate that person.

TOP TEN SIGNS THAT YOU MAY BE TRYING TO CONTROL YOUR SPOUSE

10. She has instructed your company to direct-deposit your paychecks into her checking account.

9. She keeps putting self-help tapes in your car stereo.

8. He has erased the memory of all but the sports channels from the TV remote.

7. He has suggested you wear a homing device.

6. She keeps pointing the TV remote at you and saying, "Why won't this thing work?"

5. She has your clothes laid on the bed for you each morning.

4. "Remember what happened the last time you said my mother couldn't come over?"

3. He can't shop for clothes.

2. The day after a big argument, the refrigerator is empty.

1. "Not tonight, honey. You've got a headache."

The Lifeblood

*g*rowing up in the little town of Kirchdorf, Switzerland, my (Mike's) wife, Nicole, heard this constant refrain from her English teacher: *"Sie werden nie Englisch lernen."* Translation: "You'll never learn English." How's that for inspiring confidence in a young student! But Nicole persevered. After graduating from college, she wanted to see the world and perfect her English, so she taught skiing at Mammoth Mountain, located in California's Sierra Nevadas.

When I met Nicole in Mammoth, she had an accent *à la Suisse,* but she shrugged off any teasing comments. At the end of the ski season, she took the arduous American ski instructor's certification test in English. In front of several examiners, she heard the following question: "What does friction mean?"

Nicole thought a minute, then delivered her answer.

"That's when two things frick each other."

The examiners howled with laughter. Nicole wondered what was so funny.

I'm afraid that over fifteen years of marriage, Nicole and I have had similar communication miscues, but they haven't been nearly as humorous. One that comes to mind occurred during Focus on the Family's building dedication held on a Saturday in September 1993. I thought I had told Nicole *a month before* that I would be gone all day covering the event for *Focus on the Family* magazine. But the night before the dedication, Nicole heard me making arrangements to meet photographer John Russell at 6:30 A.M.

"What are you doing tomorrow?" Nicole asked. *(You better not be working on a Saturday.)*

"I'll be at the Focus dedication, probably most of the day," I replied evenly. *(Surely, she remembers.)*

"Don't you think you should let me know that you're going to be gone for a whole Saturday?" *(Turkey. You forgot to tell me again.)*

"Didn't I tell you I'd be covering the building dedication for the magazine?" *(I'm in trouble now.)*

"No, you didn't. That's so typical of you, to forget to tell your wife." *(You're going to pay for this.)*

"OK, OK, OK."

IT'S FIRST-AND-GOAL

You won't find Eric and Jan Buherer parking their fannies in front of the TV on January 1, watching parades and college bowl games. Instead, they go to a nice restaurant at a nearby resort, real early— like around 7:00 A.M.

The Buherers have an agenda: the new year. Over café

au lait and eggs Benedict, they leisurely discuss what they would like to accomplish over the next twelve months in their spiritual, physical, and financial lives. They also define some parenting goals. After breakfast they walk around the lake, feeding the birds and talking through their plans. "It's always one of the best days of our entire year," said Eric.

Goal setting is an important form of communication. It says *I value your input. You have something important to say.* But you don't have to wait until New Year's Day to get on track. You can pick any day of the year.

It's also a good idea to plan your *week* together. Even if it's just touching base on Sunday night, going through your calendar with your spouse can head off any frustrations.

"Setting aside a few minutes at the beginning of the week has solved problems before they had a chance to develop," one husband told us. "We also prayed for each other's schedule, asking the Lord to guide our paths."

One couple said every New Year's they pulled out last year's objectives. "We were always amazed at how wonderfully God had directed our paths and carried out our short-term and long-term goals for each of our children. We did that consistently through the eight- to eighteen-year range, and it turned out to be a whole lot of fun. When the kids got older, they even joined in!"

Communication—call it talking, sharing, staying in touch, or just being a sounding board—is the lifeblood of a marriage. As much as our male egos don't want to admit it, the ball is in our court when it comes to marital communication. That is, we're the ones who feel like our allotment of spoken words is used up when we come home from work. We're the ones who emit grunts when our wives ask us how our day went. We're the ones who barely ruffle the pages of the newspaper when our wives describe the bargains they found at the farmer's market.

Willie Johnson works for the air force as a liaison officer between the brass and the civilian employees. His job is to smooth over any employee problems, which means he's constantly talking with people all day long. When Willie comes home, he's got nothing left in the tank. It's all he can do to muster up four sentences to his wife, Cilla.

Meanwhile, Cilla is dying on the vine. She *needs* some two-way conversation with Willie, not a one-sided monologue. Willie is going to have to find a second wind.

We've all heard that good communication starts with taking the time to converse with your spouse. But you might be thinking, *In our family, I can barely find a few minutes to take a shower before bed, let alone have a meaningful conversation!*

You're absolutely right. But couples must make the effort to keep the communication muscles in tone. Here are a few ideas:

• *Men, know that women are just plain different from you.* We could come up with dozens of examples, but our favorite is this one: Shortly after Todd and Tracey Thomas became engaged, they were sitting on swings at a nearby park, making small talk. Todd had a penetrating question: "Can you tell me something about yourself that you don't want me to know?"

Tracey considered the inquiry for a moment. Should she tell him? They had been dating for a year, but not all the cards had been laid out on the table. *Okaaay,* she thought, *I'll take a chance with this guy.* "You're probably going to laugh at me, but I don't like my feet. You see, I have a toe on one foot that is not the right size. See?" she said, taking her shoes and socks off.

"No, I don't see any difference between that toe or any of the other ones," replied Todd. *Women. Boy, are they strange!*

After ten years of marriage, Todd now understands why his wife made a big deal about her big toe. Her self-image was tied up in how she thought she looked to him. He probably never would have noticed—or cared—if one of his toes was oddly shaped. But not his wife-to-be.

SURVIVAL GEMS

We heard several choice quotations on developing a good relationship that were too good to keep to ourselves. Here are a few:

- "One of our themes is reminding each other to lighten up. We work hard at not taking life too seriously, because if you do, that alone can put you under the pile."

- "We're not perfectionists. We don't nag. The house doesn't have to be spotless. We let a lot roll off our backs."

- "My wife has resisted taking a getaway weekend with me. Her greatest fear was that I wanted to talk all weekend. She was right—I even had a written agenda! I finally learned to lighten up and have fun."

- "These days, I guard the home front. It's a ruthless battle to keep my career from taking more time than it should. I was real soft all through my thirties, never saying no at the office. As time goes on, the Lord's given me the strength to turn down activities that take me away from the family. I've realized that if I'm going to have anything to give my wife and the boys, I've got to cut back."

+ "The only way quality communication is going to happen is if you spend enough unstructured time together. Things come out naturally that way. We went out last week and got a burger, then went for a walk. We got more meaningful discussion out of those ninety minutes than our last official date."

+ "The challenge facing marriages today is that we do so much of everything by the clock. A friend told me his wife said, 'Pencil me in your Day-Timer for sex.' That's great she's making the effort, since their sex life has gone down the tubes, but too much fatigue and busyness prevents couples from ever having time to both be on the same page."

+ "We go through seasons where different things take prominence at different times. In recent years, we've dated a little less frequently, but we communicate more on a day-to-day basis. Our times together have kept our affection alive. The weekends away or an overnight have been the most helpful."

+ "We really recognize the season of child rearing we're in. We'll blink, and it will be over. So when our children destroy anything intimate that's happening, we'll look at each other and say, 'This is just a season.'"

+ "I give my wife the freedom to develop a close relationship with other women. If I was the only adult she's close to, then I have to meet all of her communication needs. When we lived in Ohio, I'd spend time with the kids so she could go out with her friend. That took the full weight of meeting her need to talk off of me."

+ "Ten years ago, a speaker challenged us to date our wives regularly. 'If your wife and children aren't scheduled on your weekly calendar, don't tell me they're important to you,' he said. I couldn't afford the time, but he placed such an emphasis on it, I saw how true it was. We sought out people who could baby-sit for free. I got a two-for-one coupon book and found it's well worth its weight in gold. My wife could rest assured she would see me every single week. That's developed into a time when we're involved sexually together as well."

• *If you can tell something is bugging your spouse, ask him or her about it.* Many times a husband wants to air his frustrations about his work, but he doesn't want to come across as a griper. Or a wife's frustration index just skipped off the chart because the kids wouldn't nap or do their homework, so everyone was cranky all afternoon. Slowly draw out your spouse. Ask gently but directly, "Is anything bothering you, honey? I'd like to hear about it."

Not only will you both feel better, the conversations may turn to deeper subjects, which will increase your feelings of intimacy for each other.

SPIRITUAL CLOSENESS

The old cliché "The couple who prays together stays together" can be amended to "The couple who prays together is communicating together."

There is something about letting your guard down when you discuss your prayer needs with your spouse. Whether it's a grumpy boss or feelings of insecurity, lifting up each other's burdens is a great way to lift up your marriage. "Praying together has been the most beneficial way to communicate what is really happening in our life," said one husband.

One couple read through the Bible in a year together. A wife told us she regularly asks her husband, "What have you been reading today?" That prompts a spirited discussion. "I love to talk about the things the Lord has been teaching me in the Word," she said, "which opens up doors for communicating on more than just a surface level."

• *Relearn walking.* We were surprised at the number of couples in their second decade of marriage who told us they had rediscovered the twilight walk.

"People who want to improve their marriage," said Bob Welch, "think they have to do something huge like take a two-week romantic cruise or a ten-week marriage course together. It's much smaller than that. In the last two years, the neatest thing Sally and I have done is take walks together. That sounds pretty basic, even boring or insignificant, but it has rejuvenated our relationship. We focus on each other and just talk. I don't know of any parents who can sit down and have a meaningful conversation without the kids interrupting or the phone ringing. Walks have given us a chance to communicate."

The Welches are really into this walking, cruising the streets of their neighborhood three times a week, clipping off two or three miles. Fortunately, their kids are old enough, thirteen and eleven, so they can be left behind.

"We usually walk for forty-five minutes," Bob continued. "We have two routes—one serious and one social. On the latter, we expect to stop and talk to people. For the former, Sally and I review the day and talk about the kids. There is something about walking that lets your guard down. Sitting by a fire does that, too. Think about it: You're not sitting *across* from each other like a negotiating session; you're talking to each other side by side. That makes it easier to share what's on your mind, easier to peel away the layers and get down to the nitty-gritty."

But what if you have younger children? Take them along! When my (Mike) kids were toddlers, we put one in a stroller and the other in a backpack, and we walked several evenings a week during the warm summer months. Later, when the kids were preschoolers, they loved to "lead" the way. So don't let your children's age be an excuse not to hoof the neighborhood.

TIPS THAT SAY A LOT

We could all use a few more ideas on how to make our neglected, taken-for-granted spouse feel like a special person. Try a few of these this week and see what happens.

- The notepad: Sally Custer knows how to let her husband, Terry, know that she cares. "I'll write in his date book, 'I love you', or 'I'll be waiting for you when you get home.' One time, I wrote him a letter for Father's Day and told him how proud I was to be his wife and praised the way he parented our two sons."

  Jennifer Covington once stopped by her husband's office with a present. Inside: a love note. It also made reference to the skimpy lingerie that was in the box. "I'll wear this tonight," her note said.

  Alex Baldwin loves writing little clues on notes— clues that direct his wife to hidden gifts.

  Other notable quotables: "My husband *makes* cards for me for special occasions. Though I eventually throw away store-bought cards, I keep everything he does by hand." "I never take the little handwritten notes I find in my lunchbox for granted."

- Electronics: We've mentioned before that TV can be the biggest communication killer. "For ten years we've been without a TV," said one woman. "That alone impacts how you relate to each other. It's just such a major competitor for interpersonal time, especially the man's."

  But the telephone is a close second. "Because I'm on the church board, the telephone is our family's nemesis. We could easily take fifteen to twenty calls per evening. These days, we let the answering machine do its job because 95 percent of the calls can wait."

- Breaking the routine: Finances are tight for Bobby Ray and Melissa, so they'll just put their kids to bed early so they can have the whole evening together without spending money.

  Along the same line, Elaine Minter will arrange for the kids to have dinner at a neighbor's. It may not sound like much, but it gives them ninety minutes of uninterrupted time. Oh, . . . sometimes Elaine will draw a bubble bath and ask husband Ray to communicate with her there.

  Then there's the couple who told us they invested in a hot tub. "We have deep conversations after the kids are in bed. No phones, no interruptions, and it's relaxing."

- *Even if you've been watching TV together, turn it off just before going to bed.* For instance, Nicole and I like to watch newsmagazine shows such as *Dateline, PrimeTime Live,* and *20/20.* Here in the Mountain time zone, the programs end at 10:00 P.M. Although I'm tired and ready for bed, the local news "teasers" always hook me. Lately, I've made it a point to resist their blandishments, and Nicole and I have turned off the TV and begun reading more. If a conversation breaks out (whoa!), I feel I can give her my undivided attention. I can't when the weatherman is talking about the possibility of golf-ball-sized hail hitting the Front Range.

• *Read together in bed.* Retire a half hour earlier than normal to read a magazine or some page-turner novel. A small trickle of conversation could turn into a freely flowing river of exchanges between you and your spouse.

• *Don't discuss the real important stuff after you go to bed.* "If there is something that's bugging me," said Karen Booth, "I'm usually the one who brings it up, but I've found over the years that I shouldn't begin an important discussion after ten o'clock. We're too tired to talk."

When you're tired, your defenses are down, and you're more apt to say something you'll regret in the morning. Men especially need to realize, however, that sometimes a wife just *has* to get something off her mind before it's lights out. And we heard many couples echo the biblical advice, "Don't let the sun go down on your anger."

A balance will have to be sought here. Yes, meaningful conversation can happen late at night, but keep the volume down. Save the really important stuff for the light of day.

QUALITY COMMUNICATION TIPS

We're two guys who can easily admit we didn't earn our degrees in interpersonal communication. If *you* need to go back to school to learn how to move the lips and use the ears, these tips should help.

• "Learning how to admit when I'm wrong has been hard. I've seen the importance of listening to his opinion even when I didn't want to. We learned the 'I feel' method of talking— don't correct me, don't give your opinion, and don't judge my feelings. We've learned that feelings aren't sinful. We have to stop and tell each other how we feel. When we do that, we see things about the other's heart that don't come up in the emotion of anger. He's no longer an argument to win; he's a man who has feelings."

- "We were told once to use similes when we were trying to get something across: If he played golf every weekend, I might say, 'This reminds me of the times when my dad left every weekend. I feel abandoned.' It's impossible for him to say, 'Don't feel that way!' Today, we're able to talk about our feelings all the time. Eventually, we both learned that we can't go on with unresolved conflict. Neither one of us wants to pay the price of the long-term effects."

- "A man's tendency is to fix things if the wife is going through troubles. All I want for him to do is be a counselor and listen. He's my best friend. He gives me better answers than any girlfriend does. We'll go lie on the bed, and I'll just talk it out until the puzzle starts to take form. If I start to cry, he never tells me to quit or that he doesn't want to listen. He just holds me."

• *Check with your spouse before agreeing to something.* When Hector Martinez says yes to a friend, he adds this caveat: "But let me double-check with my wife." It's surprising how often we don't think about our spouse's schedule.

• *Remember the "three Cs": communication, compromise, and consideration.* During the first five years of Fran Ognisty's marriage she communicated well with her husband, Jim, but she was a lousy compromiser. "Until I had a relationship with the Lord, I had to have my own way. He started changing my heart so I could be more giving of myself."

Compromise is a cornerstone of marriage, but it works best when both sides have aired what's bothering them. In order for give-and-take to work, offer to hear what your spouse has to say first.

Getting Off Track

Good communication also means someone needs to wave the flag when things get off kilter. Of the couples we interviewed, more than 75 percent of the women said *they* were the ones who had to swing the flag from side to side—and occasionally poke their husband's flabby midsections—when the communication was flowing only one way.

"I've always worked outside the home," said Kathleen Green, "and I think the fact that I have a job and take the lead in raising the kids makes things overwhelming at times. When life gets hectic, and I feel I'm being neglected, I'm the one who calls time out."

Young marrieds may not have discovered that men are thickheaded when it comes to tracking with their wife's feelings. We males walk through life oblivious to the little slights or huge oversights we manufacture. Donna Ronci has learned that she can't wait for her numbskulled husband to pick up the cue that her feelings were hurt.

"Jake, did you know what you said an hour ago at the dinner table really hurt me?"

"Ah, no, honey. I never had a clue." *Do I look like a mind reader? How am I supposed to know you felt that way?*

Marlou Navarro said she is the one to say to her husband,

"Hey, we have some problems." She is more sensitive to noting that their relationship is taking on water than Bob, who told us, "I am more the guy who doesn't notice a problem until I feel the torpedo hit the side."

We asked Marlou to role-play an important discussion with Bob. "Maybe I'm in the living room, and the kids are outside playing. We're finally getting to relax a little. I'll say in a nonthreatening way, 'Bob, this is what I'm feeling about our never going out anymore.' Over the years I've discovered that since Bob can't read my mind, I need to express myself in a way that will help him understand where I'm coming from. If I react emotionally, saying something like 'When are you going to take me to a movie?' he'll react defensively, and we'll get nowhere."

Bob agreed that his reflex action is to take Marlou's comments too personally. "Instead of saying, 'You're right, I could do better in this area,' I'm thinking, *Why, what do you mean I'm not taking you out enough? What about all the right things I've done recently?* I think small brush fires can turn into major forest fires because each one of us is so concerned about absolving ourselves of guilt. On other occasions when Marlou tells me she is not getting enough attention, I try to defend myself. I might say, 'I know we haven't spent as much time together as we'd like lately, but I've been coaching the kid's Little League teams and remodeling the back bathroom. You're going to have to be a little patient.'"

What Marlou is really saying to Bob is that she wants him to listen *actively* to her, to validate her feelings, as opposed to playing professor or armchair psychologist and saying this is why her reasoning is wrong.

What Do You Do When the Hurricane Hits?

When Susan Schmidt raises her voice at her husband, Walter, she is not above slamming a few doors, too. She used to bang one particular door so often that a nearby painting would hit the floor—sounds like a scene from a "Pink Panther" movie with Inspector Clouseau. "It got to be hilarious," said Susan.

Maybe you had to be there.

But are screaming spouses a laughing matter? I (Mike) have heard psychologists (not the Dr. Dobson kind) say it's a good idea to verbalize anger, to scream and let it out, to vent your spleen. You feel better afterward because "meaningful" communication has occurred, they'll say.

I'm not so sure. I've been through a few shouting matches with Nicole over the years, and I've never been proud of myself afterward. Even if I've "gotten it off my chest," I'm left with a hangdog feeling. I may have won the battle, but this was no way to win a war.

So, does raising the decibel level raise the level of discourse? Based on our experiences, screaming bouts are inevitable over the life of a marriage, but we should view them as weather forecasters view tropical cyclones.

Here's how the comparison goes: The U.S. Weather Service divides tropical cyclones into four classifications:

- Level 1—Tropical Disturbances: a low pressure area with beginning surface circulation

- Level 2—Tropical Depression: low pressure area with closed circulation and winds up to 31 m.p.h.

- Level 3—Tropical Storm: winds now between 32–72 m.p.h.

- Level 4—Hurricanes: winds more than 72 m.p.h.

We should realize that tropical storms will build up and occasionally burst into full-blown hurricanes. What that means for married couples is that if a "discussion" starts at Level 2 (fairly heated), we shouldn't escalate matters and turn the argument into a Level 3 Tropical Storm; your spouse may use that as an opening to go to a dish-tossing, furniture-throwing Level 4 Hurricane.

Instead, let your spouse vent at Level 2, and then try to calm the waters. Perhaps you can get it down to Level 1, where a more fruitful discussion can ensue.

When Nicole is at Level 2 and is ready to take matters to the Tropical Storm stage, I mild-manneredly try to steer the discussion to Level 1. Sometimes, she won't have anything to do with that. She wants me to match emotion with emotion, and (like I said) I've obliged her in the past. But my goal is to calm the roiling waters.

Things for Guys to Notice

All right, men, listen up. You may want to make a mental checklist on these items. But try to keep them in mind:

- *Your dating schedule.* If a couple of weeks have gone by and you and your wife haven't done *anything* together, you should make the preemptive strike and invite her out, even if it's just for pie and coffee at Denny's.

Unfortunately, that's not always my (Mike's) strategy. Like

a pitcher standing on the mound and peering at home plate, I'll sometimes disregard the signs of my battery-mate, Nicole. Instead of wagging her fingers, however, Nicole will say, "When can you go out for lunch?" (She's obviously past the point of waiting for me to come up with this idea on my own.) I'll stall her with my time-tested excuse: "I'm busy at work, dear. I've got deadlines this week." (Hey, I have deadlines *every* week, but don't tell her that.)

If she continues to press me, I'll commit to a lunch date the following week, knowing full well I can cancel later after her mood has passed.

I can't believe I get away with this as often as I do, but the sad thing is that my stonewalling hasn't been good for our marriage. Lately, as I've realized what I'm doing, I've agreed to same-day or next-day lunch dates, even if my trusty PB&J sandwich is already stashed away in the Focus fridge. And you know what? Those are *always* our best lunches.

For those who don't like a hit-or-miss approach, you can try to emulate Dr. George Fitzpatrick, who uses the super-organized approach: Once a week he takes his wife out for dinner. Once a month he spends the day with her. Once a quarter they go for a weekend getaway. And once a year they take a week's vacation together without the kids.

Man alive!

TOP TEN LEAST POPULAR HUSBAND-WIFE DATES

10. A romantic evening listening to her Don Ho cassettes

9. Arnold's latest "Terminator" flick

8. A greasy, gut-bomb burger at "Joe Bob's Barbecue," followed by pool at Mr. T's Highland Park Bowl

7. A heart-to-heart conversation with the principal at your teenager's school

6. Watching hubby go for a new personal best at the all-you-can-eat place

5. A Living Will seminar

4. The motorcycle parts swap meet

3. An exciting evening at the Monster Tractor Pull

2. Your best friend's annual Super Bowl party

1. A four-hour trip to a time-share presentation in the middle of the desert

---

• *Bring her flowers.* Or chocolate. Or something she likes. My (Mike's) wife *loves* flowers, and I try to buy them for her as often as I can, but they are expensive. In the Rockies it's hard to find a decent bouquet at the supermarket for under six bucks.

I figure, however, that's the cost of doing business, because if I ever get into Nicole's doghouse, she's sure to throw this teary-eyed statement at me: "And not only that, but you *never* buy me flowers!"

"But honey, remember two weeks ago? I brought you a bouquet from Safeway."

That usually buys me some time. But this flower thing goes a long way back for the two of us. I remember my first visit to Switzerland, when Nicole and I had had a disagreement. To make up, I went into a local Swiss supermarket and bought a big bouquet of bright red carnations.

With my left arm swung behind my back, I presented the flowers with a flourish. She was standing outside the supermarket with her mom, and they both started laughing tears.

"What's so funny? What did I do?" I asked.

"These are funeral flowers," said Nicole.

How was I supposed to know?

• *Back to the future.* Finally, how many times has this happened to you? You're sitting in a restaurant, and you notice an older couple sitting in a "two-top" next to the window. For the entire dinner, they barely utter a word to each other, silently lifting their forks to their mouths, quiet in their thoughts. *They must have run out of things to say to each other when Jimmy Carter was president.*

Is that going to happen to you and your spouse? Will you run out of things to talk about? Not if you believe— with full conviction—that quality and quantity communication is the lifeblood of a marriage pointed toward a Renaissance.

DATING IDEAS

When's the last time you and your spouse went on a date, just like in the good old days? Candlelight dinner, soft music, continental cuisine. Just the two of you. Here's what some couples had to say:

- "The only rule we had for a date was it had to be some place where we could sit down and talk. Our goal was to hook up emotionally, that's why we didn't go to movies."

- "To keep our communication skills developed, we get away and do different things we enjoy. The last couple of years we've gone to plays. We talk about our impressions, what we learned, and what we liked or didn't like. We learn more about each other by hearing what we think. *Les Miserables* moved us. It was one of the best plays we've seen."

• "During our second decade of marriage, we had a date every Wednesday night. Sometimes I didn't want to go. I was tired or didn't want to leave the kids with a baby-sitter. But he insisted, and I'm glad he did."

• "One of our rules on date nights was we couldn't talk about stressful issues or things we knew would be a conflict. We had to talk about mutually edifying things, so we took turns picking the week's subject. We also took turns picking the place to go and not telling the other one. We did that for ten years. Yes, we had a few nights when we stayed home, but it had to be a really good reason not to go. And no one else could go with us, either. That was one of the main ingredients that kept us communicating and caring about one another."

• "We live by our calendar. Good intentions don't happen. Weekly dates have to be marked off. The same for weekend getaways. We schedule them three to six months apart. It always seems to help, getting away just to have fun."

• "In the early years when we were broke, my parents would come over, give us twenty bucks, and tell us to get lost. They'd baby-sit the children . . . and we took off. That was great! We plan to do the same for our kids."

• "When you fall in love with someone, you learn to enjoy doing things she loves. These days, we attend musicals, plays, and symphonies—things I never would have done before. I can honestly say it's been fun. Once, when I took her to the symphony for Mother's Day, she wanted to leave, but I wanted to stay!"

• "If you go away for a few weekends each year, try something unique—don't have sex. We learned to enjoy each other without any physical expectations. A few times, we just checked in and slept for twelve hours because we were so exhausted."

- "Bill would like to go out to dinner and have a romantic evening out, but we don't have the money. He would like to take a romantic interlude—a weekend away—but he won't organize it. What we do look forward to, however, is the time we are together in a car. We drove to New York City to see some friends one year. (That's 210 miles one way.) We looked forward to that five hours in the car—just the two of us. Did we talk? Did we ever!"

- "I made a big commitment to finding several baby-sitters I could trust and call. That took work. We didn't have grandparents around to help out."

- "On her birthday I rented a limo. We drove around awhile before we did dinner and a movie."

- "When I turned thirty, I mentioned to Tom that it was a big deal for me, and I wanted it to be memorable. He called all my friends and organized a progressive dinner. He borrowed a friend's Mercedes, and he even bought a corsage for me!"

Great Expectations

*P*arked outside of a McDonald's, I (Greg) sat with my wife in our '78 Chevette. The cold, soggy French fries and the rainy Seattle afternoon matched my mood.

"Elaine, I'm just tired of living."

Though I couldn't believe I actually said those words, they were the only utterances I could get out. After eleven years of marriage, I was deeply dejected with the way life was going.

"I just wish the Lord would take me home," I continued, sounding more pitiful by the second.

My wife had that *"I'm sympathetic, but if you think you've got it as bad as I do, you're dreaming"* look in her eyes. I ignored her and plunged ahead, laying out all my frustrations. Children were a good place to start. The boys were three and one, and as little children do, they were monopolizing our lives. Troy was recovering from his third and final surgery to correct a birth defect, and Drew had just emerged from being a demanding, colicky baby to a demanding, whiny toddler.

My job? Well, the work was good, but my paycheck *barely* met the monthly budget. I was a Youth for Christ worker dependent on the support of friends and acquaintances. Plus, I was having trouble recruiting enough volunteers for my youth ministry. From the other end, my boss continually reminded me he had high expectations.

Romance? We hadn't dated in months—no money. It seemed like we didn't have time to even talk. Elaine and I both walked around in a continual state of exhaustion. Sex was a chore—even for me!

In this weary state, I needed some attention and sympathy, a little TLC. Fortunately, Elaine didn't jump into a tirade on how *her* life was going. If she had, we both might have agreed to drive the car off the Evergreen floating bridge into Lake Washington!

Parenthood, marriage, work—life in general—wasn't going like I'd hoped. I wish I could say I immediately snapped out of my blue funk and returned to being the upbeat person I'd always been (and am today). But I didn't. What I did do, however, was go back to basics: I prayed, read my Bible, and took solace in some of my favorite music. One song that particularly reached me was a Steven Curtis Chapman song called "Wait on the Lord." I kept cuing it up every time I hopped in my car. Then I continued the slow, everyday plodding through some years that hadn't come near to meeting my expectations.

I look back on that day with a lot of embarrassment. Life may have thrown me lemons, but *I wasn't in the mood to make lemonade.* Instead, I wanted out—completely out. But that's not what I really wanted, of course. I wanted life to change, to get better. And it did . . . about two years later. Now it's been seven years since that day, and I'm enjoying life more than ever before. My boys bring me a happiness I never expected, and my marriage is coming out of the Dark Ages. There's a Renaissance in sight.

Was my ignorance, immaturity, and wrong expectations an aberration for a Christian man? Though perhaps a little more melodramatic than most, it's hardly unusual. Let's hear Mike talk about his early years.

Like everyone going into marriage, I (Mike) carried certain expectations. I expected Nicole to have the same temperament I do (I'm evenhanded and mellow; she's Mount Vesuvius), go to bed at the same time (I'm pooped by 9:45; she's still raring to go), and spend money the same way (I love to save; she loves to shop).

Lest you think I'm a male chauvinist, let me say that I view all those descriptions of Nicole as positive attributes. Sure, she has a temper, but she's a mom who makes things happen. Even after the kids are in bed, she's still baking cupcakes for the kids' classrooms, knitting a ski hat for Andrea, or preparing her German tutoring lessons. And though I'd like to see her curb her expenses, she doesn't spend much money on *herself.*

TOP TEN EXPECTATIONS THAT ARE USUALLY NOT REALIZED IN MARRIAGE

10. The frequency of sex during the honeymoon is an indicator of what hubby can look forward to in married life.

9. He'll get a high-paying job so that she can stay home and shop for a living.

8. She'll cook just like Mom.

7. I'm marrying my wife, not my in-laws.

6. We'll never fight or argue because we'll be too busy being in love.

5. The wife will never nag the husband for leaving the toilet seat up.

4. She'll love to go to the driving range three times a week after work.

3. He'll take a daily shower.

2. She'll maintain her physique.

1. That he'll even come close to maintaining *his* physique!

As for the marriage, I assumed two things: We'd have kids someday, and we were hitched for life. But I didn't know how *long* a time that can be. (We're at the fifteen-year mark now, and if we live to the end of the average life expectancy, we still have thirty-five more years to go!)

Pretty routine stuff, I agree. But let's have some fun. Let's compare some modern-day marriage expectations against *reality*:

Roles

The expectation: My wife is a wonderful homemaker who keeps the house spotless. When I come home each evening after a hard day's work, she greets me at the front door with a kiss. She sets our well-behaved children in front of the TV, and then leads me to the bedroom. After our "late afternoon delight," I relax in the La-Z-Boy with a cold drink in hand, today's newspaper on my lap, and ESPN2 dominating my big-screen Mitsubishi. What a life!

The reality: I arrive home an hour after dark to a house in total panic. My wife, who works part-time, is struggling to keep her patience as she cleans out the dishwasher, loads wet laundry into the dryer, and helps the kids with their homework. When I walk into the kitchen, she announces that the kids are starving. "It's your turn to cook the Hamburger Helper," she says.

Work

The expectation: The company *really* appreciates the job I do. Not only does management proffer regular raises, but they tell me that I'm being groomed for vice-president.

The reality: I'm glad to have the job I have; I just pray the company doesn't eliminate it during the next round of "downsizing." I was handed a 2 percent pay raise last year, but that was gobbled up by the hike in the company's medical insurance program.

Housing

The expectation: The two-story colonial with the white picket fence backs up to the fourteenth fairway.

The reality: We're still saving for a down payment. (Or, if we already own a home, now we know why it's called the "money pit.")

Romance

The expectation: Flowers from my hubby every payday.

The reality. Flowers from my hubby every six months. (OK, every nine months.)

Kids

The expectation: What an honor and blessing it will be to have children of our own, made in the image and likeness of God.

The reality. Rebellious teenagers who hate church, tolerate family vacations, and aren't interested in college.

Money

The expectation: There will always be enough.

The reality. There never is enough.

Sex for the Husband

The expectation: When the lights go out, my wife is turned on. Her appetite for sex is insatiable.

The reality. She just wants to talk.

Sex for the Wife

The expectation: My husband will never be in a hurry.

The reality: He's hurrying.

Did you see yourself in any of those scenarios? Perhaps, but you'd agree that those expectations were a tad *unrealistic*. Don't get us wrong; expectations can be good. Like goals, they can motivate a couple to strive for intimacy, provide for a better future, and raise well-mannered children. But unrealistic expectations in the second decade of love can keep a couple in the Dark Ages. Here are some expectations we heard in our interviews that probably never should have been there:

"My Spouse Will Meet All My Needs"

Jennifer Norton went into marriage looking for her husband, Bruce, to fulfill her. "I was expecting my mate to satisfy every need I had, but God is a jealous God. No man is going to fulfill me, and the Lord never meant for any man to do that, anyway."

Comment: We are all human beings, which means we come to marriage with all the foibles and imperfections of any other person. Anyone assuming the spouse will be a reincarnation of a chivalrous knight or a lovely maiden is setting himself or herself up for disappointment. Rather, our identity should be in Christ, the only one who *was* and *is* perfect. He alone is able to speak the truth about who we are and how important we are to him.

Women are particularly susceptible to expecting their husbands to meet their needs. That's why *female friendship* is so important. Several wives with low-expressive husbands (in other words, talking-impaired or verbally challenged) learned through the years their man couldn't provide them with *all* the adult interaction they needed.

"My Life Will Improve with Children"

Maybe, maybe not. "People told me that life would be wonderful after my first child was born, but that was a bunch of baloney," said Maxinne Laver. "I had more trouble adjusting to our child than to marriage."

For another view, Jonathan Eastley told us, "Our kids have been a 'met expectation' and have put much joy into our lives. It's a privilege to be a parent. I love to have someone to laugh with and be goofy around."

Comment: To everything, there is a season, and that verse from Ecclesiastes (3:1) never seems more apt than when raising children. Much of the time you're in an attitude of gratefulness that God would trust you with children, but then there are those days. . . .

"My Wife Will Stay Home and Raise the Kids"

Wait a minute! That's no longer a given. First of all, some mothers *have* to go back to work to keep food on the table. Or, they make more money than their husband—or have a much better health-care plan. Some are more career-minded than mommy-driven.

Comment: Even if this topic is handled in premarital counseling, that doesn't mean you'll be thinking alike five or ten years down the road.

When a couple is ready to have children, both partners should express their expectations on these issues: How many? How far apart? Will the wife return to work full-time? part-time? How do you feel about day care? Is the wife working for the money or to have a daily break from the pressures of motherhood? How much money will we actually net after all the expenses are totaled? Who will stay home when the kids are sick? Who will choose the day care or baby-sitter?

You'd be surprised at how many couples fail to confront these questions.

"We'll Always Have Enough Money"

Remember the saying, "Two can live as cheaply as one"? Well, you can forget that old chestnut. A 1990s version might be: "Four are going to have to learn how to live on one paycheck."

"I never expected to have financial problems," said Jannine Wolcott. "I never expected to even think about it and even discuss it with my husband."

Added Robin Engel: "I thought for sure I would be financially comfortable like my parents. But my husband and I barely live paycheck to paycheck. I never thought we would be on such a tight budget, but that's what life is like."

Comment: Growing up, I (Mike) had this rose-colored view of finances. I thought a regular job would always cover rent, groceries, and gas money, with something left over. If I wanted to buy something, then I'd curb my purchases for several weeks. The money would be there next month. Wrong! It's a struggle to make it to the end of the month with *anything* left to put into savings.

"The House Will Always Be Clean"

Katy Lowen always felt she had to be the perfect homemaker: carpets vacuumed, venetian blinds dusted, windows washed, rooms picked up, and kitchen spotless.

Once the kids arrived, Katy and her husband, Jacob, realized that keeping a clean house fulfilled the law of diminishing returns. "We decided that the house had to be clean enough to be healthy, but dirty enough to be happy," said Katy. "That allowed me to be comfortable when people dropped in and things weren't dusted. But I struggled with that, since I wanted the house neat and tidy when Jacob came home."

Comment: My (Mike's) wife, Nicole, is a maniac about a

clean house. She scrubs the house from top to bottom Mondays and Fridays—and it was clean to begin with!

"Honey, the house looks great," I'll say. "You don't have to clean tomorrow."

"Oh yeah? Have you seen the bathrooms?"

Guys, we can do a lot to help out. Time studies in recent years have shown that while women are spending *less* time housecleaning these days (thanks to the rise of working moms), women still do twice as much housework as their spouses. Together, assess the total needs of the family and see who's doing what. Are you both comfortable with the division of labor?

"My Husband Will Be a Leader"
Martha Fuller assumed her husband, Geoff, would be a strong head-of-the-household-type who wakes up Saturday morning and says, "It looks like a great beach day. Who's going to make the tuna sandwiches while I pack the car?"

"I learned Geoff is not that type," said Martha. "He asks me what I think before we decide anything. Funny. I wanted somebody who would be king of the house, but I got somebody who had a servant's heart."

Comment: Be extremely thankful for who you've got, Martha.

"Since We'll Know Each Other So Much Better, Our Communication Will Improve"
Laurie Campbell told us the art of conversation has been the most unrealistic expectation for her. "As my husband got older, he clammed up more. I thought when you got mar-

ried, you truly became best friends. But we never experienced that 'best friend' conversation I longed for."

Comment: Although Nicole and I sometimes finish each other's sentences, she will *always* be much more verbal than I. I'll admit that I often do nothing more than grunt or nod my head to keep the conversation going. I have to resist that behavior.

"Dreams Do Come True"

Did you ever want to run your own successful small business? Buy a house with a tennis court in the backyard and a lawn so big you need a riding mower? Be able to pay for an overseas, summer missions trip with your family without draining your savings or asking everyone you've ever known for support? Ever want to combine career and motherhood without losing a beat?

Comment: Don't stop dreaming.

"I Thought Our Sex Life Would Not Taper One Iota Since Our Honeymoon"

We're going to deal with sex in chapter 9, so we'll hold our comments on this expectation. But if you know any couples in their second decade of love still going at it like two suntanned honeymooners in Hawaii, can you contact us? We'd like to write a book on them (although it would likely have to be categorized as fiction).

It's the Attitude, Stupid

Tim Flannery walked down the church aisle behind a wheelbarrow full of expectations. Growing up as the son of an uncommunicative father, Tim was one of those earnest folks who was sure *his* marriage would be different.

"When I got married, I expected Jenny to dress a certain way, be a good cook, and act in bed the way I wanted," said Tim. "We went through the usual initial stages of exciting love and passion."

But then child number one arrived before the first anniversary. Twenty months later, the Flannerys brought home a second child from the hospital. Tim couldn't understand why his wife was tired all the time. "Jenny and I have never had much warmth in our relationship, so our marriage reached a crisis point where several of my expectations were not being met," said Tim. "I tried to be patient with her. For her part, she was darning my socks and focusing on our little family, but I didn't think it was working. We were fine as long as we were trying to achieve a goal, but from an emotional standpoint, there wasn't a real closeness. My thoughts like this went on for several years because I was never satisfied with her, no matter what she did."

Right about the seventh year of marriage, Tim was talking with one of his young children, and from the mouth of babes, he heard the following statement: "Did you know, Dad, that we can go through life happy or sad?"

Wait a minute! That applies to me, too, Tim thought.

"That was it. No divorce, no looking back. I made a decision at that time to cherish my wife. That meant I was going to focus on every good quality she had, not her bad ones, and I was going to put any negative thoughts out of my mind. God doesn't bring up negative thoughts—Satan does."

What We Learned

Over the next year, Jenny was able to relax as Tim let up. "She became everything I wanted her to become," he said. The marriage experienced a Reformation.

An important principle is involved here. Expectations should not be too lofty, especially in the first decade of love. Instead, couples should be looking to serve each other—rather than be served—as the household falls into a certain rhythm. He shouldn't wait for her to ask if he can help clean the dishes; he should just do it. She can cook his favorite meal, not because it takes thirty minutes longer, but because it shows that she cares about the hard work he puts in at the job.

Coming Back to Earth

Expectations are often sky-high in the first decade of love. Age has much to do with it; idealism is in its highest orbit, and well it should be. We leave school hearing that our horizons are limitless, that we can be who we want to be.

"The thing about expectations is that people could have told me anything when I was young, but I still wouldn't have understood," said Patty Faulkner from the safe harbor of twenty-eight years of marriage. She and her husband, Will, married young—Patty was just nineteen. "Any advice at that time wouldn't have meant much to me," she said. "I wouldn't have received it with the same mature heart that I had when I was, say, thirty years old."

Reality has a way of chipping off chunks of the dream, as we mentioned before. If we happen to be married, as many of us are in the late twenties and early thirties, we look for the nearest scapegoat: the spouse. He or she becomes the punching bag.

Another important point is that many of us grew up in broken homes, and having a divorced parent as a role model—no matter how heroic he or she was—can certainly *lower* one's expectations for a happy and successful marriage.

In addition, many of us far into the second decade of love were married before premarital counseling came into vogue. Talk about flying blind. My (Greg's) only advice on sex came from the pastor who performed our ceremony. "Get your business done quickly and get out of there. It won't be comfortable for your wife." That was it! (Fortunately, practice has a way of improving these types of areas.)

If you've been frustrated by life's turns, not only will you have to forgive your mate, you'll likely have to seek forgiveness *from* your mate. Only when you can come to that point will you be able to experience a Reformation. You're going to have to say to yourself: "This is the person God has given me," or "This is the job God has provided," or "These strong-willed children have been entrusted to me." Turn those circumstances over to the Lord. Fred Hardy did.

"I always thought that one of the neatest things that could happen to me was that if I married the right person, I would be marrying my best friend," said Fred. "It took a few years, but today I feel a real sense of support when I come home after a tough day. I can unload my day on her, and she can unload on me. I really appreciate that she listens and is my best friend. During a tough week, I might get a card in the mail from her at work. I didn't expect it, but I cherish having that type of relationship where she can pick me up when I am down."

If you're looking for a Renaissance as it relates to expectations, Fred's found it. He and his wife are learning that a true marriage is where one tries to outdo the other in serving and building the other up.

Couples who allow unrealistic, even selfish, expectations to dominate their marriage are short-circuiting God's plan for their lives. Thoughts of an early exit from the marriage during the inevitable ups and downs are always planted by the father of lies. Instead, keep in mind these two points:

+ Nearly all couples have had wrong expectations about how life should turn out, just like you.

+ You can get back to reality. Lowering your expectations is a start, but also realize that God is attempting to do big things *in you* and *through you.* How does he do it? By allowing you to experience real life with all of the highs and lows it brings.

A WIFE'S EXPECTATIONS

+ "The thing I remember about my early years of marriage is that all of a sudden I had someone around twenty-four hours a day. That was a big change for me. When we married, I was twenty-six and he was thirty-one, but after six months, I found it hard to believe I was going to be married to this guy for the rest of my life. It was such a big adjustment."

+ "You know, the starry-eyed love disappears, and if that is all you married on, there is nothing left."

- "After you're married and have a few kids, you think, 'I've done everything I've wanted to do. What else is there to look forward to?' Plenty, as I've learned."

- "I wanted to marry a godly man whose priority was God's will. Thankfully, I did marry a man whose heart for God has never wavered."

- "Sex was a disappointment. It took us a year before I was doing anything more than servicing him."

- "I wish I had understood more about the differences between men and women. These days, when we're getting ready for bed and my husband's not talking to me, I don't think that means he doesn't love me."

- "I've been married nearly twenty years, and all of my expectations have been met. I was not demanding economically. If I had wanted a wealthy husband, I would have struck out."

A HUSBAND'S EXPECTATIONS

- "We never set a lot of goals. The Bible says to be content, and that was our goal."

- "The world glamorizes men's sexual fantasies. That's not how women react to you. When you make a grab, don't expect them to respond! Women just won't jump on us."

- "I thought marriage meant Candy was supposed to be my servant."

- "To be honest, I kind of jumped into marriage. The only thing I knew was that I loved Linda, and I wanted to spend the rest of my life with her. But I didn't realize back then how much I would grow in love with her and how good my life would be. My love seemed to grow as I became more responsible, as I could provide for her, and be a good steward of what God has given me."

• "I don't have to put on any airs for Sally. She knows my strengths and weaknesses, and most of all, I can be myself around her. With other people, that is not good enough. I appreciate the opportunity to be natural."

7

How Quickly Time Flies . . .
How Easily Weeds Grow

*f*or many couples, the first ten years of marriage are full of goals: landing a good job, scrimping for the down payment, buying new furniture, adding on a room—and raising 1.8 kids. Yet beneath the surface ominous rumblings are beginning. Any number of marital problems—romantic neglect, bad communication habits, different outlooks on child rearing, problems with in-laws—can begin to take root during the Dark Ages. These weeds are stubborn and— like a dandelion that pops up between sidewalk cracks— very hard to pull up, as it was for this couple.

Time to Call Time-out

From all appearances they made a perfect team. When Sherry Harper met Jeff Phillips, he was a backup catcher for the Oakland A's. Tall, handsome, and a graduate of Stanford University, Jeff was no dumb jock. Sherry, for her part, was a beautiful young woman with high cheekbones and a china-doll complexion that suggested she could have been a New York fashion model. A trim brunette with curves in all the right places, Sherry wasn't an airhead, either.

Their storybook marriage began in the early eighties. Eighteen months later their first child, Scott, arrived on the scene. This redheaded tornado was a pistol; he had no problem staying up until Jeff came home from the ballpark at midnight. In the wee hours, his sandpaper screams kept his zombielike mom awake. Another brother and sister were added to the lineup.

Tired and cranky, Sherry did her best to cope. But like an absentee homeowner who fails to weed a flower bed, she let her house go. In the old days, their abode could have been featured in *House and Garden*. Soon, a fatigued Sherry had a different mind-set about housecleaning: *mañana.*

Her husband, however, was Felix Unger to her Oscar Madison. He liked a meticulous home with everything picked up and in its place. "When you take something out, it should be returned where you found it. That makes for an orderly house," Jeff constantly reminded Sherry.

A typical day for this young mother began with her climbing out of bed, slipping on house shoes, leaving the closet door open, walking downstairs, taking out a tin of Yuban coffee, leaving the pantry doors open and the coffee can out, carrying several cereal boxes to the kitchen table, stacking the dirty dishes in the sink, going back upstairs, changing into day clothes, and leaving her nightgown on the unmade bed. And it was only 8:25 A.M.

When she took a shower, she left her clothes strewn and the wet towel on the counter; ditto for the hair dryer. That had been her practice even before the children came along. Now, she fell *much* farther behind. The hurdles to keeping a clean house were insurmountable.

"When I came home after a long day, I could see this messy trail she had left," said Jeff. "Naturally, I would say something about it, always mentioning that I couldn't live like that. I am a list- and task-oriented person who likes to check things off, accomplish goals, get things done, and move on to other things. Sherry wasn't."

Jeff took the extreme measure of bringing in a maid to do some housework, but that was only a Band-Aid. Slowly, over time, he began to resent Sherry's sloppiness. *Why do I have to come home to this mess? And what if somebody drops in?*

While Jeff felt indignant, Sherry felt helpless, and she withdrew into her shell. Their Thursday evening "date nights" fell by the wayside, and to keep the peace, they stopped saying anything meaningful to each other. Often, they went to bed angry, which meant their sex life tapered off to practically nothing.

The Phillipses kept up a brave front to outsiders, but underneath the surface resentment smoldered like the fuse on a cheap Fourth of July firecracker. From the sixth to the ninth years of marriage, the Dark Ages dominated their relationship.

Meanwhile, Jeff poured himself into the children. Every free moment, he stood in the cul-de-sac and pitched batting practice to Scott and Patrick. After that, they shot baskets or went to a nearby tennis court to practice forehands and backhands.

"You see," noted Sherry, "it's socially acceptable for a husband to spend all his spare time with the kids. Jeff used the kids as a distraction so he wouldn't have to spend time with me. How could this Superdad be criticized for spending every minute with the kids? It's the same trap for a wife with a workaholic husband. How can you fault him for working so many long hours? He's only trying to provide for his family. Hey, at least he's not going out and drinking with the boys."

The couple was at an impasse. Several times Jeff talked to his pastor, who thrust some resources into his hands. Individually, they sought the Lord in prayer about the health of their marriage, but they were still at a stalemate.

"We needed some kind of divine intervention," said Jeff. "I can see now why marriages fail. If you're going through a stressful period, especially if you are from a dysfunctional family where there has been divorce in the past, you begin to see that as an option. For me, it was not an option, even though we were at each other's throats."

It took a good friend to break the logjam. Hugh Gardner couldn't help but notice that Jeff and Sherry weren't very friendly to each other. The stress and tension were beginning to show in both of them.

One afternoon Hugh sat them down and offered an olive branch to each. "Whatever it takes, you two have got to get out of here and talk to each other." He offered to look after the kids the following morning so Jeff and Sherry could go for a long walk along the Pacific Coast shoreline.

When the two arrived at the beach, Jeff—drawing on his baseball background—gently suggested some ground rules: No yelling or screaming, and the other person had to be accepting of whatever was said. *They had to hear each other out.* This was a time for honesty. Too much had been building up for years.

Jeff stepped up to the plate and made himself available. "Just tell me everything, and I'll listen," he said.

"OK," said Sherry, taking in a breath before hurling the first pitch. "Everything has to be perfect in the house, including me. Well, I'm not perfect, and the house will *never* be perfect, either. I would like you to love me unconditionally, for who I am. I think everybody wants to be accepted for the way they are."

"Fine," said Jeff. "Tell me more."

That was a big moment. He wasn't defending himself at all.

So she continued. Sherry said that she hated to see what was happening to their marriage. She confessed that she felt as though she got a bum deal during the early years. When Scott was born, she suffered sleep deprivation the first two years of his life. Most days she couldn't put two sentences together. She wanted to keep a clean house and please Jeff, but she was exhausted.

"I have stopped doing things I liked to do, like going out to movies, visiting museums, horseback riding, and having coffee with girlfriends. I've done this all for you and the kids. When we do have company over, it's always your family or your friends."

That morning they talked for four hours—letting out every bad thing that had been eating at them for ten years. "It felt so good to get it all out, and feel semiclose to each other again," Sherry said. "It had been a long time since we'd talked about our feelings."

Jeff listened as he had never listened before. They held each other, oblivious to any onlookers. The beginning of the Reformation had come. It was time to put several difficult years behind them and walk out of the Dark Ages.

Sherry reports that a year after their soul-searching morning, their marriage is experiencing a Renaissance. "It's not that we don't get mad at each other, but knowing each of us wants the marriage to work makes the present so livable. We still have our bad days, but we get over them because we've learned how to show love to each other. We've also gotten more involved in church, which has been a steadying influence for us."

What We Learned

Jeff and Sherry's struggles illustrate a common plight for busy couples. Small communication weeds were allowed to grow in the first decade of marriage until the relationship was choked by a garden of stinging thistles. Taken alone, each weed is fairly minor. Plant them together in the same plot, however, and you've got some major tilling to do.

Though the Phillipses should have taken that coastal stroll years earlier, they took the right step that Saturday morning. The key was Jeff's making himself vulnerable. He flashed an important sign to Sherry: *I'm going to listen to you, and I'm not going to defend myself for a change.* By inviting her to express her pent-up frustrations first, Jeff won Sherry's trust.

Another key was their commitment to each other and the marriage. Once the process of weed clearing began, they saw immediate progress. That encouraged them to clear their weed-infested garden and plant the right relational seeds.

Everyone's Got 'Em

Since weeds pop up even in well-tilled gardens, you don't need a Ph.D. in horticulture to know that marriage is fertile ground for emotional weeds to take root—especially in the all-important first decade. To keep them from overtaking the whole plot, weeds have to be pulled—regularly.

The problem: In the first decade of love, couples like Jeff and Sherry sometimes lack the ability to recognize marital weeds. Weeds can grow up around them so slowly that they never notice them overtaking the marriage. Consequently, these weeds form deep roots. Left unattended, they can contribute to *wedges* in the second decade.

Time-out for two quick-and-easy definitions:

Marital weed: A slow-forming situation or attitude usually caused by poor *communication habits.* Taken alone, they seldom damage a marriage irreparably. (Example: a spouse who lets problems build up for a month until the "perfect" opportunity to talk arrives.)

Marital wedge: A *situation* or *circumstance* that often grows up around a number of unattended weeds. Until these weeds are pulled out of the relationship, communication and intimacy (a Renaissance) are nearly impossible to achieve. Resentment and discouragement often set in. (Example: a spouse who can't or won't talk about deeper problems for fear of a negative response.)

Of course, every garden and marriage has weeds. Though we can't prevent them from growing, we *can* prevent them from contributing to wedges that damage the relationship or split the relational concrete.

Sounds as though we need good weed killers, or individuals willing to break a sweat as they hoe the dirt. Here are a few garden-variety weeds common to many marriages. If you see any of these in your relationship, do two things: Recognize it, and then form a strategy to pull it out of your marital soil.

"My Battery Is Different from His"

The Weed: One partner doesn't respond in a caring manner when the other's energy level is depleted.

When you were in high school, you probably ran on a fifty-volt battery; that is, you had enough energy to burn the candle at both ends for as long as you wanted. After you married, you might have moved down to four D batteries—but still plenty of power for long days and active nights.

But when children entered the home, something happened. In the middle of the night, someone switched the wife's batteries and decided not to tell the husband.

Though men are slow to notice, occasionally we'll catch on that our wives are no longer marching around the house like the Energizer Bunny. If we're smart, we'll alter our expectations and start picking up the slack.

Or, if we're dense to our wives' depleted energy reserves, we will get on their case, as Jeff Phillips did. *Hey, I'm knocking down twelve hours at the office and spending Saturday in the garden. Why can't she do her share?*

Eventually, a dim light begins flickering in the husband's head (usually after getting hit upside it). He makes an amazing discovery: *My wife's batteries aren't the same as mine, nor are they as strong. Maybe I ought to make some adjustments.*

But if a man is self-centered, he won't have a clue that these energy weeds are turning into a wedge.

Marie Williams knew the color of that weed when she saw it, although her husband, Joel, was oblivious.

"At the twelve-year mark we had a crisis," Marie told us. "The demand for my time and energy was getting to me.

Our kids were young, and though I never worked outside the home except for short periods of time, I stayed busy. Among other things, I helped other moms by being the room mother they couldn't be.

"But the physical demands of having the house perfectly straight, preparing three meals a day, and canning fruits and jelly finally got to me when my husband kept harping that his sexual needs weren't getting met. I said, 'To blazes with it.'"

Joel's problem was twofold: (1) He thought that since he was raring to go, she should be, too, and (2) he believed that if his wife didn't want sex with him, she didn't love him—and he told her as much. Forget that she was showing her love for him by doing *everything* else. Joel was concentrating too much on *his* needs.

Marie finally got it across—in counseling—that she wasn't withholding sex on purpose; instead, she was too tired at 11:00 P.M. to participate because she used up all her energy to keep the *family's* needs met.

"Before we started counseling, Joel believed with a straight face that when he was home, I should always make time for him. Naturally, that made me feel guilty," Marie says. "I thought our problems were my fault. But talking with a counselor allowed me to blurt out that I felt Joel was too demanding. The counselor sided with me! Joel's inconsiderate behavior was the problem."

Joel's reaction? "I have to agree with the counselor. In fact, the realization caused me to break down and become more sensitive to what my actions were doing to my wife. Sure, it was humbling, but I was grateful and relieved that someone finally pointed that out."

Their marriage healed quickly, Marie reports. If Joel was a one on the sex-sensitivity scale during the Dark Ages, he's an eight in the Renaissance.

What We Learned

It's tempting for couples to wait until a weed grows three feet high before finally realizing something better be done. And then instead of attacking the weed, they verbally attack each other. Too many times, however, they ignore the growing weed altogether.

Ideally, Marie should have informed Joel that her batteries had been switched. Then Joel should have taken the hint. Both Joel and Marie admit, however, they relied on a game married couples play: Read My Mind! When they realized they were never going to win that one, they listened as a counselor pointed them to another game: Let's Talk.

The Comparison Game

The Weed: Playing second fiddle to spouse #1.

We interviewed only two couples who were remarried, which is a proportionally low sample for the 1990s.

The odds of having a successful marriage go down dramatically with each successive marriage. Among the potential problems is husbands and wives wondering deep down what their spouse thinks of them vis-à-vis spouse #1 (or #2, or #3).

Dennis Hood was anxious to please his new bride in every way he could. Sure, it was her second marriage, but this was a new start, right? From the beginning, however, doubts plagued the young man's mind. *Am I treating her nicer than the other fellow? Am I a better provider? Would she ever leave me, too?*

As Dennis searched the Scriptures for solace, he began to realize that Satan will bring up every negative comparison to cause him to be dissatisfied with his mate. "I had to concentrate on the positive because if I didn't, I knew my mind was being fed things by the enemy," said Dennis. "The other thing is that by focusing on the negative and not cherishing my wife, I was opening myself up to temptations. In many ways, love was a decision for me."

Helen Gray was head over heels in love when she married a widower whose first wife had died tragically from cancer, leaving two young children behind. But Helen came into the marriage with some excess baggage, which only fueled her second-wife insecurities. Growing up, her alcoholic parents—their tongues loosed by drink—browbeat her, often telling her she was worthless. Consequently, she was as tightly wound as a flea market watch. Although Jerry rarely mentioned his first wife, Helen assumed her new husband was always comparing her with his dead spouse.

If Jerry rearranged the dishwasher to fit a few more dishes, Helen thought she was a poor housewife. If he didn't rhapsodize over the baked chicken, she thought she was a lousy cook. To top off her problems, they lived in the same town as the parents of Jerry's first wife. Ever the dutiful son-in-law, he felt he couldn't cut them off, especially since two grandchildren were involved.

At first, Helen stayed home when Jerry took the kids for a visit. She felt his former parents-in-law wouldn't want to talk about their deceased daughter if she was there. One afternoon Jerry returned home and told Helen she had it all wrong—they would *love* to have her visit. Life goes on, they said, and they understood why Jerry remarried.

"I'll never forget the day when I realized Jerry's in-laws accepted me totally," said Helen. "Knowing they love me freed me to love them."

What We Learned

A mind is a horrible thing to waste, but it sure can work overtime when circumstances propel it to play the comparison game. In order to survive, marriage needs four cornerstones of security, not second guesses.

In Helen's case, loved ones who went out of their way to show unconditional love conquered a multitude of fears and helped her draw closer to her spouse—and their grandchildren.

Them Fightin' Rules

The Weed: You or your spouse never learned how to fight fairly.

Dozens of couples we interviewed lamented that before they married, no one taught them to fight fair. Here are some of the comments we heard:

- "When we argue, we accuse. We can't seem to keep our feelings parked in neutral. We're both so competitive that we want to win the point."

- "We're afraid to express opinions to each other because the other gets so defensive. All that does is bottle up the truth until it explodes."

- "Early on, I used to let things seethe inside. When the explosion occurred, my husband would accuse me of planning the entire episode."

- "My husband and I shy away from conflict. He likes being happy and looking at the bright side of things. That's usually good, but he tends to deny when things are bad."

I (Greg) can certainly relate. My parents divorced when I was thirteen, but for two years leading to the breakup, it was "Friday Night Fights at the Johnsons'." I can still recall that horrible feeling in the pit of my stomach when my parents started raising the roof. I'd head off to my room and turn up the radio so I couldn't hear the mean things that were said. Two years after the divorce, Mom married a three-time loser—and a wife beater—and that gut-wrenching feeling returned. (Fortunately, that marriage lasted only a few months.)

What did I learn? *To avoid conflict.* Though I didn't know it at the time, when I married Elaine at age twenty, she was also an "avoider." We were a perfect pair for our first seven years of marriage; I can't remember fighting one time. But when Troy and Drew started running the halls, Elaine and I had regular "disagreements" on discipline issues, plus some other things that were starting to bug us.

When I was ready to talk, I'd sit Elaine down and say, "I have something we need to discuss." She knew what that meant. In her mind I was preparing to lob a few hand grenades at the way she was disciplining the kids or planning our weekends. She felt her self-image was under attack.

When it was her turn to confront me, she'd let it build up and then just "throw up" all over me. Nothing loud or mean, but . . . illogical. The problem: My male mind wanted reason and calmness. Her female emotions needed to vent.

What We Learned

Eventually, Elaine and I learned over eighteen years to accommodate and compromise, but I wish we had started discussing the way we should handle conflict much earlier in our marriage.

Don't force your spouse to read your mind. Talk about the type of home you grew up in. Was it one confrontation after another, or did family members go out of their way to avoid conflict? Were disputes handled with a lot of gestures and pointed remarks, or did Mom and Dad sit across the kitchen table and hash out their differences?

After setting a few ground rules for confrontation that you can both live with, take time to pray together if this issue is a deep weed. Many people struggle with anger and don't know how to express it appropriately. When that happens, anger not only has the potential to damage the marriage, it can also leave ugly scars on impressionable children—who can pass this dubious legacy to the next generation as well.

COMMON WEEDS

Time to pay attention here. Do you recognize any of these weeds in your marriage?

- "We were constantly taking each other for granted."

- "Manny is such a helper and a people person. The problem is, he serves other people before the family."

- "I tend to make the family miserable because of my inability to be content."

- "Jeremy's not a real communicator. He says what he wants, then it's over with. That frustrates me. I love to sit and talk, but he gets bored. About our fifteenth year I realized I couldn't change him. That's the key in dealing with a husband who is the silent type."

- "I let urgent things push out important things."

- "Every night after fixing dinner, I need to escape to my bedroom and have some time away from the kids. For a while, my husband was understanding when I'd close the door and take a hot bath. Then he got frustrated that I'd disappear at 7:30 while he had to put the kids to bed. He thought I was abandoning the family."

- "I assumed that after you got married you could say things like, 'Gee, I don't think I like you doing that.' Then your spouse says, 'Oh, OK, I'll change.' Life doesn't work that way."

- "We got married in the infatuation stage. Our early pattern was the silent treatment. We'd disagree over what we would do on the weekend, how we would spend our money, and who to socialize with. Then we'd go several days without talking at all."

- "Our marriage taught us what quid pro quo means. It means 'I'll scratch your back if you will scratch mine.'" (But not before.)

- "I approached marriage with lists of things to get accomplished, but relationships don't work that way."

- "We're traveling in different directions during the day. I deal in millions of dollars with sixty-eight employees;

she deals with potty training and exploding washing machines. Seeing things from each other's perspectives is essential—especially me to her."

• "I came into my marriage thinking I had to be right. I didn't value a woman's perspective at all."

Weed-infested Theology

What keeps a marriage free from three-foot weeds? We believe the key is having a solid, clear fix on the problem between you and your spouse—you're sinners! If you don't keep this condition in mind, weeds will run rampant in your marriage. You may not notice them until it's too late.

The best way to illustrate this idea is to look at what happened between God and man. As Christians, we believe the Bible teaches that our sinful nature makes a close relationship with God impossible. Logically, then, if sin separates us from God, why wouldn't it separate us from each other?

Well, how did God deal with the mess Adam started? He had four choices:

• He could pretend our sin didn't exist.

• He could destroy the human race.

• He could leave the universe and start another colony of humans in some other galaxy light-years away.

• He could do something that would free his unique creations from the terrible consequences of their sins, which separated them from him. (Yes, he chose this one!)

What must we do in response to God's choice?

We need to recognize our sinful condition, repent, believe that Jesus Christ died to save us from our sin, and receive his forgiveness into our lives. Then, as we learn to follow him, we need to turn away from our desire to think the universe revolves around us . . . and realize who he is. Only through humility and submission can we attain the intimate fellowship with God that we were intended to have.

If we use the above lesson as a metaphor for the points we are trying to drive home in this book, it reads something like this. . . .

The spiritual Dark Ages for the individual are those years when he or she doesn't know the extent of God's love (by ignorance or by choice). Either the person hasn't heard or refuses to accept the fact that God would actually come to earth in the person of Jesus Christ and die on a cross to pay the penalty for sin.

A spiritual Reformation occurs when a person—beyond simply believing in the existence of God—actively chooses to pursue a *personal* relationship with Jesus Christ, who promises salvation to those who believe in him.

This step allows a spiritual Renaissance (remember, it means "rebirth") to occur, which allows a person to enjoy the fruit of the Holy Spirit.

How does all of this relate to marriage?

Just as human sins are unavoidable, so, too, are weeds that grow in marriage. If a couple doesn't understand where the weeds are coming from, then their problems will always remain a destructive mystery. Disillusionment, incompatibility, and uneasiness will occur during the Dark Ages as one or both partners act on their sinful nature by trying to take charge.

How can a husband and wife deal with this control issue in a practical way?

Rex and Sharon Petersen finally discovered what worked for them.

"By the time we had been married about ten years," Rex says, "Sharon and I had subtle but clear rules for the power game and often locked horns for control. This created a marriage made in hell."

That's not exactly where the Petersens wanted their relationship to be. "Unless we were willing to come back to the place of humility—God's humility—and lay down our own agenda, then our marriage problems were never going to be fixed," said Rex.

"Most partners want their own way and don't mind hurting each other to get it. We discovered that only when you lay down your rights do you get what you really need."

The same impetus that causes people to allow God to save their souls can inspire couples to save their marriage. "But you can't save a marriage through any gimmicks," said Rex. "It will only stave off the inevitable. The weeds that can choke a relationship have the ability to grow that big."

Sharon says after the first decade of marriage, the tension finally challenged them to talk, think, and pray through their basic belief system of what was wrong with them—and what God wanted them to do about it. Their rallying cry became, "If we get separated, if things go dark, if we're seriously off-kilter . . . then the agreed-upon rendezvous is at the Cross."

"For over twenty years, that's what we've done," Sharon says. "When I disappoint, hurt, or grieve Rex, he can say, 'It's time to meet at the Cross.' That statement has helped save us from short-term bitterness and long-term resentment."

Why Christian Marriages Get into Trouble

If one of the married partners doesn't have correct beliefs about sin, then they may try to handle the problems by using their *own* power, not God's.

Yet when it's realized that the same thing that opens the doors to heaven can also open the doors in marriage, the Renaissance years have begun.

We recommend this immediate plan of action: Make sure you're not a halfhearted Christian sleepwalking through life. Do you do religious things that give the appearance of Christianity, or have both of you turned away from self-rule and become followers of Christ? If, as a couple, you can honestly say that Jesus Christ is at the center of your lives, that's when you'll finally have the ability to be mutually submissive to each other.

We spoke with several wives who admitted they had submitted for years to their husbands, but their husbands were not submitting to Christ. Each situation was fraught with problems. "It became almost a spiritually abusive situation," one woman told us.

How does it happen?

Just as Christians use the God-given freedom to take advantage of Christ's goodness, a husband or wife can take advantage of the spouse's acts of submission. It's repugnant to God and repugnant to the spouse.

One counselor said: "Couples with major problems who eventually learn to take their problems before God and each other *always* make steady progress. They'll have their struggles, of course, but they will see consistent, positive change because they're under the direction of the Holy Spirit."

Closing Thought

After several weeds become a wedge, what should your response be? Our next chapter talks about the most common wedges couples face today.

8

Attacking the Wedges

*i*t wasn't quite Woody versus Mia, but Tom Ballard wasn't about to lose to his wife, Lainie. They were locked toe-to-toe in an intense combat of the wills.

The challenge: The room was cold. The wood floor was colder. They were both in bed. The overhead light was still on . . . and the switch was clear across the room.

"Honey, would you please go turn out the light?" Lainie asked in a tired voice.

"Me? You were the last one in bed," Tom responded gruffly. "Why should I get up?"

"Because it's cold out there, and I'm comfy."

"You should have thought of that before you climbed into bed."

"But I've been with the kids all day long. I've got to get some sleep."

"Oh, brother, here it comes again. What have I been doing all day, sitting in a hot tub watching *Gilligan's Island* reruns?"

Silence.

Finally, five minutes later Tom says, "Are you going to get up and turn off the light, or not?"

"No, that's the man's job."

"Fine."

They both lay on opposite sides of the bed. They closed their eyes . . . and the light remained on. It stayed that way most of the night!

So what happened?

"Lainie finally had to get up in the middle of the night to go to the bathroom," said Tom. "She turned off the light. I won!"

"Tom Ballard, you just annihilated your wife and made her feel like a doormat. What are you going to do to celebrate?"

"I'm going to Disney World!"

Thus ended another battle of wills at the Ballard household. "For years, control was the big thing with us," Tom says. "We'd try to jockey for position and change the other person. We're both strong-willed *[yeah, we noticed]*, so for her to give in, she needs some distance. She won't give in in the heat of a disagreement. I'm the jerk because I like the competition. I'm very determined."

Turning out a light in a cold room probably isn't a big deal in your house, but even simple episodes between a husband and wife can become a wedge. It's safe to say wedges—or circumstances that divide married couples—are common in every household.

The biggest wedge we discovered in our research was *sex.* Of course. (But we're not going to talk about s-e-x just yet. Hang in there. We'll get to it!)

Whether it's specific wedges or adapting to a spouse's personality, couples need to examine what pushes the wrong buttons in the relationship. It's easy to use your spouse's personality flaws against him or her—much in the same way Muhammad Ali continually jabbed at Joe Frazier's eyes. No one enjoys being a punching bag, including your spouse.

Anyway, here's what our couples said were the *big* wedges:

The Money Thing

Children don't come cheap: Braces, sports, clothes, food, presents, hobbies, music lessons, and entertainment are stuff youngsters deduct from the monthly budget.

Do you see any marriage land mines that could come up while you try to find enough money for these essentials during the child-rearing years? It's more sad than funny, but many couples we interviewed didn't—and struggled because of their lack of insight.

"It's a Man's Job"

"My wife, Nina, is much more disciplined than I am," said Bob Anders. "But my pride wouldn't let her hold me accountable in making money decisions. Not in what we saved or how we saved—or even in day-to-day stuff I wanted to buy. I thought it was my right to do what I wanted. I didn't respect her advice, so I didn't follow it."

Gee, Bob, sounds like you're the type of guy who wants to keep things in control. What happened? Did everything work out for the best?

"I wound up getting us in about six thousand dollars'

worth of debt that didn't honor the Lord . . . but it did validate my wife! I had to apologize to God and Nina."

Bob learned a costly lesson. It took them two years to dig themselves out of that financial hole. Today, they *mutually* control the money.

What We Learned

Money—or the lack of it—is the second-biggest wedge for many couples. It can cause the relationship to stay in the Dark Ages when couples fail to realize each others' strengths and weaknesses. A man should drop the pride if he can't do the job and admit God may have given him a wife who is more disciplined. God's good at forging individual weaknesses into marital strengths.

Financial Freedom

Money management is a big deal for Arnie Blauser.

"When we first got married, Betty would buy things; then I'd criticize her purchases. She'd shop, and I'd grind my teeth. We got to the point where money became an issue every week. It was emotionally draining—for both of us."

How did they solve it? Once a year they took time away from the kids and did some goal setting. Money management was part of the agenda.

"We switched to a 'cash-only basis,'" Betty says. "Arnie and I set the budget, and we decide how much I should have for food, clothes, and household stuff. Today, he never has to ask me how much things cost."

Once they agreed on a monthly number, Arnie quit worrying. "She'd show me a new outfit she bought for one of the kids, and I didn't feel the need to micromanage her."

Betty says the expectation for the last ten years is that they will stick to the budget unless they mutually agree to allocate more. "There have been times I've overspent on clothes, but I have his trust. I don't want to let him down. There's real freedom in how we're doing things now."

What We Learned
Money management doesn't have to be stressful if you can learn to become trusted members of the same team, rather than insecure competitors vying for control. If your income is consistent, relieve the potential stress by planning ahead. Though 90 percent of couples do not work from a budget, if you can take some halfway measures—such as tracking your expenses for several months—you'll get a handle on your spending. For those who have kids, you already know what financial stress is all about. Let us point you toward some Christian financial experts (Ron Blue, Larry Burkett, Austin Pryor, and Wilson Humber) and relay the most difficult-to-follow advice in the world: Learn to spend less than you take in.

The Discipline-of-Children Thing
As I (Greg) mentioned earlier, Elaine and I waited seven years—and never fought—before we had kids. After our two boys took up residence, however, it seemed as though discipline was the main source of conflict.

Since I grew up in a passive home, I rarely took the initiative to do the right thing. I'm about as laid-back as they come (Yorkey is a close second), but Elaine had to deal with an energetic toddler named Troy racing through the halls all day. She'd practically wear out a wooden spoon every week. (OK, I'm exaggerating, but we're talking a strong-willed boy here.)

But when Troy pulled his hyperkid act in my presence, I didn't have it within me to confront the lad. It was out of character for me to play Mr. Disciplinarian.

Elaine, in our periodic bedtime "discussions," convinced me that I had to toughen up to keep in step with what she was doing—and what was right for Troy.

Is Dad Really Home?

Can you believe it? Children are born without an instruction booklet that could help us straighten them out when they start "malfunctioning." As with me, several couples admitted that one of them was clueless when the kids were acting bad. That happened in the Huber household a lot, too.

"One night my eight-year-old son, Josh, arrived home late from hockey practice. He was tired, unreasonable, and disrespectful," said Jeannette. "My husband, Steve, is the silent type, but in this instance, I purposely sat on my hands, hoping he would handle it. When the situation worsened, he didn't know what to do.

"Right or wrong, I stepped in and resolved the conflict. I knew disciplining wasn't my husband's strong point, but I wish he would get with the program. It's a struggle to know whether I should stay in the background or let him learn by trial and error."

What We Learned

Who should take leadership when it comes to discipline? The quick answer is it's a fifty-fifty proposition, but life rarely works out that way, if only for the reason that Dad is at work all day. When he comes home, however, and still leaves the disciplining to his wife, he is abdicating his leadership role as a father. And if she's two steps ahead of him on disciplining the kids, will she dominate in other areas as well?

If a team approach isn't taken, the kids will lose respect for one of their parents. Or, the parent having to wear the black hat all the time will resent that role. It's also a poor example for the kids since we tend to parent as we were parented.

Realize, too, that it's no character flaw if your spouse doesn't know *how* to properly discipline; it's simply an unlearned skill. Buy a copy of Dr. Dobson's *The New Dare to Discipline,* and ask your spouse to read it. (If your husband is not the reading type, the book is available on BookTraks. Also, Dr. Dobson has taped numerous broadcasts on this topic, which can be requested through Focus on the Family. Your spouse can listen to them during his commute.) With all the wealth of information out there, don't let excuses carry the day.

Drop-in Dad

As a young child, Coreen Noble lived through rejection from her parents. When she became a mother, she was determined her children's lives were going to be different. But her two toddlers did what small children are prone to do—take control!

"I wanted my kids to love me," she says, "so for a long time I let them walk all over me. I was the ultimate servant-mother, so I spoiled my kids.

"My husband, Wes, traveled in his job. But when he was

home, he saw what was happening. He'd try to come to my rescue by getting tough with them, but sometimes I thought he went overboard. Then I'd get mad at him in front of the kids, trying to defend them. Naturally, he was hurt by this lack of respect. Though we always made up, it took me awhile to learn that his role as father of the house needs to be affirmed, not torn down."

What We Learned

If the man's work includes out-of-town travel, the couple needs to understand a few things. On the home front the wife has flown solo with the kids, so she's ready for a break. Meanwhile, the husband is usually bushed from the business trip, but she's expecting him to pick up the slack around the house.

Our advice to women: Don't expect much the first night he's back. Sure, you deserve a break today, and he should help out. But it's unrealistic to expect a dad who's flown through several time zones to pick up the family rhythm the first hour he's home.

Our advice to men: You're going to have to suck it up. Sure, you missed your connecting flight at O'Hare and arrived home three hours later than expected, but your wife's been shouldering a huge load in your absence. Walk in the door and say the six words a mom likes to hear: *What can I do to help?*

A Common Cry

Should parents spank their kids? Is corporal punishment akin to child abuse? To spank or not to spank was a wedge in more homes than we thought.

Some Christian homes view spanking as a barbaric holdover that produces "violent" kids. I (Mike) have heard this sentiment from a vocal minority of *Focus on the Family* readers whenever we publish an excerpt from *The New Dare to Discipline*.

The majority of families, however, understand that a small amount of corporal punishment—a thump on the fingers of a toddler, a mild smack to the behind of a preschooler—is just what the doctor ordered when a young child *knowingly* tests the limits of bad behavior. An example would be when a youngster crosses the street after you forbade it or a grade-schooler steals change from her mother's purse.

Strict Does Not Mean out of Control

Take Rick Lennon, who comes from a military family where strong discipline was the order of the day. Consequently, he's always been strict with his four kids.

His wife, Beth, however, was yelled at when she misbehaved. So Beth screamed a lot at her four kids. Later, when she had a chance to cool down, she realized that part of the reason she was yelling was because she was mad at Rick. *His* discipline worked, and hers didn't.

Beth's anger at Rick continued until this incident occurred. "When my oldest son was four, I got so mad I threw him against the wall," she said. "The next week he had the flu and had to go to the doctor—a Christian friend of ours. He asked me about the bruises. They weren't serious, but he reinforced what Rick had been trying to tell me: *Don't let things build up. Handle the problem the moment it occurs.*"

What We Learned

The way you were disciplined as a child is probably the way you will discipline. That's not always good. Before each stage of your children's lives, talk through a strategy for discipline.

Don't just move ahead, expecting your spouse to follow your lead. A united front is always stronger.

Champion Manipulators

Where do children learn the skill of playing one parent off the other? Good question, because nearly all children become adept at this as they grow older.

Kristi White is convinced she's the mother of the all-time champion manipulator: her son, Jeremy. "For years, my son has watched my husband, Allen, and me discuss what we should do when Jeremy asks us permission to do something. Then he usually plays one against the other, and we've *really* got a problem. Allen and I learned the hard way that we need to be in agreement whenever Jeremy pushes one of our buttons."

What We Learned

Children learn early that if they can't get one parent to go along with what they want, they can hit up the other parent. By simply being aware of this tactic, couples can avoid the Dark Age grief of letting that cause conflict between the two of them. Be on the same page when it comes to tough decisions. Then if there's a disagreement, discuss it later out of the child's earshot.

The Major-Decision Thing

While most couples keep a united front when it comes to big decisions (a job change, buying a new car, choosing to have the wife invest her time at home), this area can divide couples faster than a forgotten anniversary.

Rich Easton wanted to move to a nicer house, but his wife, Jarnice, didn't think they could afford it.

"We'll be strapped," she told Rich.

"Don't you think I know that?" replied her husband. "Well, somebody has to make the decision around here, and I'm the man of the house, so I'll decide."

Emotion prevailed over reason.

Today, the Eastons are house rich and cash poor. They have two kids who need braces. The oldest child was having problems in public school, so they had to transfer him to a Christian school. To make up for the shortfall, Jarnice is working as a waitress—tough, on-your-feet work for any mom. She resents having to work so hard outside the home—where her children need her.

What We Learned

God sometimes uses the "irrational" logic of a marriage partner to protect the family from harm. When it comes to major decisions, it's always better to first, pray together, and second, wait until there's a unanimous vote. If not, resentment can enter in. Worse than that is the spouse who has to pay the consequences for the other's (usually the man's) inability to wait.

TOP TEN REASONS WHY SHE ALWAYS WINS THE ARGUMENTS

10. Who wants to go into overtime?

9. She's just like her mother!

8. I'm a grown man, and I like to eat!

7. She initiates discussions while I'm trying to watch the game.

6. She always changes the subject and starts talking about my shortcomings.

5. She only thinks she wins.

4. Halfway through the spat, he forgets what they were arguing about.

3. Practice makes perfect.

2. Men typically prefer the "high road."

1. You know why.

Holidays, Vacations, and the In-Law Thing

About 30 percent of the couples we talked with mentioned that these "three amigos" had affected their marriage. Because they didn't anticipate problems in these areas, wedges cropped up. Some actually threatened their marriages.

Blood Is Thicker than Water

Even though no one in her family was a believer, Belinda Mercer always had a strong attachment to them. But how much time should the Mercer clan spend with her side of the family?

"For years, we took all of our vacation time to visit her relatives," said Belinda's husband, Larry. "Those two weeks weren't really the vacation weeks *our* family needed. Besides, her relatives weren't Christians—in fact, they were pretty messed up. That meant we were spending time with pitiful people."

Whoa! Belinda and Larry sat down and discussed the situation. They decided to see her relatives every other year, and if her parents wanted to see them, they were welcome to visit anytime.

The upshot is that when they broke the every-year-at-Grandma's pattern, Belinda wasn't going to see her parents as often. Larry sensed this, and before Belinda could say anything, he offered to send her on a plane once a year so she could visit her folks.

What We Learned

Don't let extended family times rule your household. Though the pressure might be intense, talk through what is fair to everyone before committing yourself.

Along with that, realize your spouse may share a deep bond with family members. Respect and encourage frequent contact if your budget and time allow it.

Cutting In-Laws

"The first few years of marriage, my mom, brother, sister, and cousin were merciless to my wife, Christina," remembers Eddie Espinosa. "My oldest sister isn't a Christian, so she used her disregard for religion as a way to get under my wife's skin. My cousin was just plain cruel.

"It's kind of a sick type of love. My family likes to slice-and-dice each other. I finally put my foot down. I wrote letters, called them on the phone, and even told them in person that I will not tolerate this abuse! My wife really appreciated the way I stuck up for her."

What We Learned

Don't sit idly by while a relative pokes fun at your spouse. It's tough for the victim to respond to someone from the other side of the family. *Always* publicly defend them. If more correction is needed later on, do it in private.

Homesickness

I (Mike) am going to get personal and tell you the *biggest* wedge for Nicole and me. No, it's not money, although that would rank a close second.

It's her homesickness.

As I mentioned before, Nicole is Swiss. She will always be Swiss (as she is fond of reminding me), and if you had to have a straight answer from her, she would prefer we lived in Switzerland. That's where her parents live, plus her brother and his family, all of her relatives and longtime friends. (And we haven't even talked about how she misses skiing in the Alps yet.)

If you are living hundreds of miles away from extended family, you're well aware of the heartache that can cause.

Right around our sixth year of marriage, Nicole grieved for her homeland. Our two children were toddlers, and they were growing up without Nicole's parents seeing them during their "cute stage." And her brother was starting his own family. This Dark Age wedge was especially dark for us.

I remember having dinner right about that time with some German friends, Dieter and Marlene Fieberger. The subject came around to homesickness, and Marlene—then in her late forties—told Nicole how homesick she felt after she emigrated from Germany in the 1960s.

"The only thing that helps is time," she told Nicole. "I've been here for nearly thirty years, and there have been occasions when I thought my heart was going to break. But I hung in there. You can, too."

And she has. In the last five years, we've been able to make two trips to Switzerland, which have helped immensely. In the interim years, her parents have come to the States to see us.

Air travel has certainly made the world smaller, but we're like millions of couples who live half a continent away from "dear old home." It's too far to drive, and it's costly to fly a family of five from Seattle to Atlanta, for instance. We're like many couples who move to another region of the country because that's where the work is. We live in Colorado Springs, and I have one of the best jobs in the world editing *Focus* magazine. So what's our family supposed to do?

What We Learned

Time will heal, as I mentioned, but having kids will help, too. Why? Because you'll be establishing your *own* traditions with them. At Thanksgiving, for instance, you start passing around a small basket filled with Indian corn. The kids ask you what you're doing. You reply that they're supposed to take a piece of corn and describe what they're thankful for in the last year. You're starting a new tradition.

Or, you take summer camping trips with your kids—just like you did with your folks. Again, forming your own traditions is a wonderful antidote for homesickness.

The way I view it, if you're living more than a thousand miles from loved ones, you probably won't have the time— or the money—to fly home more than once a year. You're probably going to suffer bouts of homesickness. Can your parents visit you?

The Job Thing

Both of us have lived part of our lives in Oregon. I (Greg) was born in Portland and grew up in Eugene; Mike graduated from the University of Oregon. We agree on one thing about "God's country": It sure is tough to make a living in Christian journalism there.

Perhaps you're living in a part of the country where the economy is lousy. That can leave a desperate feeling in a parent's throat. So when Steve Humphrey told us how he conducted a nationwide job search after trying for seven years to build a financial planning firm in Klamath Falls, Oregon, we listened to how his job search stressed out his family.

First, he sought the Lord's direction, and after three days of prayer, he felt he was being pulled to solicit a job from Ron Blue and Larry Burkett, two well-known Christian financial counselors. It's hard to get hired in Georgia (where Blue and Burkett live and operate their companies), so Steve and his wife, Annette, took the plunge and put their house on the market. It sold quickly (unusual for that depressed state), and they moved to the Peach State. They lived with Annette's folks to get their bearings; Annette was pregnant with their third child.

For *eleven* months they shared the same roof with his in-laws while they waited and interviewed for the right job. Finally, he landed a position.

We could tell you much more about Steve's laborious job search, how difficult it was waiting for the phone to ring, the humbleness he felt while he waited for an interview, or the strains on the family's financial health.

"I never want to do that again, but those eleven months were a time when Annette and I gained strength together," said Steve. "How? Because of the trial itself. I was forced to communicate more with her, and the job search gave us a different day-to-day perspective on what's really important. We spent a lot of time talking about serious things, such as the future of our family. We also talked about how the Lord was leading us. When I finally landed that job, we knew the trial was worth it."

What We Learned

Men derive much of their self-esteem from their work (Why else do we ask, "What do you do for a living?"), so if the job isn't doing well, men have a tendency to clam up and keep it inside, if for no other reason than they want to "protect" the wife and kids.

Steve, at a vulnerable time, made himself vulnerable to Annette and made her feel like a *partner* in this job search. They used the experience to bring them closer together.

The What-Fulfills-Mom Thing

We spoke with three types of women:

- 1. Those who love being full-time, stay-at-home moms; the boy-I-can't-wait-to-have-another-child type of women

- 2. Women who feel full-time motherhood is great, but their whole identity isn't wrapped up in it

- 3. Those who recognize that being a good mom is the godly thing to do, but who had a great, fulfilling career before children and want to do more with their time than simply be a mother

Naturally, these are generalizations, and our intention is not to put any type of motherhood down. God created us with different temperaments and gifts, and *vive la différence!* We're not saying one type of mom is better than another; we're just explaining what we observed. But we want to relate some stories about how each type of mother affected her marriage and draw some general principles from these illustrations.

The first group of moms, who put all of their energy into the kids and the home, derived their sense of fulfillment from how good a job they did. But while the kids were happy and the home was a source of pride, the husband often had to fight for attention. You can imagine the potential wedges that occur if the wife doesn't have the energy to connect with her husband. And what will the marriage be like when the kids have left home? Will he get any attention then? For unperceptive mothers, it will likely depend on how close the grandkids live.

The second group of moms have accepted this season of motherhood with good cheer, and they are doing all they can to raise good kids and keep the home in order. At the same time, they know their husband needs attention, so they do the little things to communicate that he's still number one. While this may look like the ideal way a marriage should be run, wedges can surface here as well.

Moms whose attitude falls into the third category may leave the most room for wedges to form. Why? The husband wants someone who will take good care of the kids, but he also desires someone who will pay attention to him. Yet this type of woman usually finds her deepest sense of purpose outside the home, whether it's a career, ministry, or community service.

Again, the potential problems are obvious. The wife doesn't mother like the husband's mother probably did. Though she loves her spouse, he's not her reason for living (which is good). She gravitates toward those things that bring *her* fulfillment, but that doesn't mean she doesn't love her husband and kids. She's just wired differently.

What We Learned
You *can* have good marriages and well-adjusted kids with a wife from any one of these categories. But if the wife is at either extreme on the spectrum in mothering personalities (too much the "earth mother" or too much the "tolerating mother"), two things have to happen: First, her mothering/wife style has to be recognized and admitted. Second, the husband must have the freedom to wave a red flag whenever he needs to talk. Expectations are going to go unmet unless both husband and wife are in agreement about roles, time, energy levels, and what the husband's needs are.

Professional Ministry
The stress from being in full-time ministry is often more than a marriage can bear. We spoke with several pastors and their wives who faced critical times when the church seemed like more of a mistress than a ministry.

"The early years were the toughest," says Anthony

Hernandez. "Running a small church is a one-man show, much like a small business. You're in a continual balancing act of two top priorities: work and family.

"In my head and heart, I knew that Sienna and the kids should come first, but I loved what I was doing. Seeing people come to Christ was very fulfilling, but it can eat you up. I had a tendency to get out of balance. I wouldn't notice it; then my wife would start feeling left out, lonely, and probably resentful. Guys in other professions have the same kind of pressure.

"Whenever I'd get too busy, she would start registering her frustrations. She would say, 'I feel like the church is another woman.' She's said that a number of times over twenty-five years. Sometimes I felt it was unfair, but it would alert me to start looking at what I was doing. Sure enough, I'd check my calendar and see that I had been working seventy- to eighty-hour weeks. She's rarely been unfair about her complaints. Nearly every time she's spoken up there has been an unbalance."

What We Learned

Men don't realize that wives often have the gift of being a gyroscope. Wives need to feel the freedom to help the man know when things are out of balance in business or ministry. As we said in our first book, *"Daddy's Home,"* the most important hours of the day are when a man is home with his family. Though there will be times in a man's work life when pushing the pedal to the metal is important, if seventy-hour weeks go on for months at a stretch, the marriage will suffer. Paying that price isn't wise.

Whether you are in full-time ministry or just highly involved in church work after office hours, neglecting your family to do "the Lord's work" can put a wedge between you and your spouse. Wives, too, can become overinvolved in ministry. We'll more fully address the challenge of church obligations versus family obligations in chapter 14.

Time Doesn't Come in a Bottle

Before the marriage, young, unmarried couples usually spend all of their spare time together. Then after the honeymoon, some men feel as though they've made their "catch," and their interests turn to other horizons. Women can feel this way, too. After a few years of marriage, this potential wedge usually materializes.

"I'm a high-need person," says Corinne Busslinger, "and I readily admit it. I'm a puppy dog and would follow Bryan around and be at his heels. I need people."

That was a big problem for the Busslingers. While Corinne needed people, Bryan wanted privacy and space—especially after a long workday. Corinne's also a wife who believes a man shows his love to her by how much time he spends with the kids. Bryan thinks his family should show him their love by letting him relax on the golf course.

Fortunately, the Busslingers have excellent communication skills. But what would happen if they didn't regularly—and calmly—talk through these differences in personality and expectations? You might see a weekly dose of hurt feelings, blowups, "the silent treatment," no intimacy, and two people wondering if they should try to stick it out or start over with someone who's a "better match."

What We Learned

The Busslingers recognized the problem of not having enough time together early on. They talked it through on dozens of occasions and made the right changes before the wedge had a chance to divide the marriage.

Many couples, however, let that behavior fester before dealing with it. Since marriages and families need T-I-M-E to thrive, the spouse who senses that his or her mate is escaping shouldn't be shy about finding out the reason— even if the spouse is emotionally or physically absent. There usually is one.

How God Uses Wedges

Circumstances or poor decisions made in the daily grind of life—as well as during times of crisis—can leave couples in the Dark Ages, especially if there isn't a foundation of commitment.

While no one likes problems, keep in mind that God is using them to firm up your marriage—to draw you closer together. He can also use wedges to draw us toward him as we learn to look to him for guidance and help.

If you slam an eight-pound steel wedge into a round of oak, one of two things will occur:

- The wedge will simply move the tissue of the wood tighter together; or

- the wedge will split the wood in two.

We chose to use these illustrations of marital wedges to

underscore the point that while wedges can—and often do—split marriages, they can also bring a couple closer to God—and each other.

Does that include the biggest wedge that came between the couples we interviewed—SEX?

You betcha!

9

Tonight's the Night

W e're going to talk about sex, aren't we?"
Although we heard that question from our interviewees several times, each occasion still caught us off stride.
Going in, we thought we'd have to ease into this subject since
it's ah, you know, kinda personal.

But hey, we're in the nineties, and people didn't mind
talking about their sex lives to strangers. (Understandably,
the friends and acquaintances we interviewed were more
reticent on this topic. We'll be telling a few stories on
ourselves in this chapter, and there's *no way* we're doing it
in first person. It's Pseudonym City all the way.)

So, what was the big thing we learned? That sex begins in
the kitchen, right?

Well, yes and no.

"In terms of physical intimacy," said Derek Dayton, "I
was expecting more spontaneity. I can be ready to go in a
moment's notice, but not my wife. It took me awhile to

learn that sex sometimes does begin in the kitchen when I do little things for her."

But getting sex out of the Dark Ages during the second decade of love isn't as simple as peeling potatoes for half an hour and then sweeping the aproned wife off her feet for thirty minutes of heated passion. "My sex life is an outgrowth of *all* the other things happening in my life," said Andrietta Ellis. "It's the most vulnerable thing a woman can do, and my husband's treatment of me leading up to sex will either make it a joy or a pain for me."

Oh.

Making sex something you *both* can look forward to takes work. Tons of factors came into play that all serve to prevent or delay real sexual satisfaction.

Here are a few:

For Women

- Did Mom talk about sex favorably or unfavorably during the teen years? (Or, was there any discussion on the subject at all?)

- Was there any sexual, physical, or emotional abuse growing up?

- Was there premarital sex or heavy petting with other guys before marriage?

- Was there premarital sex or heavy petting with her future husband before marriage?

- Did the wife communicate with her new husband what she liked and didn't like? Or did she let him try to read her mind?

- Before children came along, was sex a duty? (If it was, then sex is *really* a duty after the kids arrive!)

- How does the wife feel about her body? Is she ashamed of it?

- Does she have trouble reaching a climax?

For Men

- Did he learn how to *communicate* with girls from his dad, or ogle girls with friends?

- During his teen years, did his peers or pornography warp his view of what women really want?

- Was there premarital sex or heavy petting with other women before marriage?

- Was there premarital sex or heavy petting with his future wife before marriage?

- Did he try to please his wife before himself in the early years of marriage? (Thus showing he wasn't sexually selfish.)

- Did he roll over or turn on *The Tonight Show* after sex was done? Or did he continue to love his wife by talking, touching, and hugging? (Thus showing he wasn't sexually selfish.)

- Did he make deposits into his wife's "emotional bank" before making a withdrawal from her "physical vault"?

- Was he demanding or understanding after the kids were born?

- Does he "remind" her until she yields? Does he take the joy out of sex?

- Is he always in a hurry to satisfy himself?

These and other issues can often determine whether the sexual relationship will *ever* exit the Dark Ages. Ask any old married couple about the subject, and they will reply, "It was a learning process." A satisfying sex life, they agreed, broke down into these three attributes: communication, understanding, and patience.

Battling a Sordid Past

What happens to the marriage bed when one spouse is sexually experienced but the other isn't? Sometimes, the emotional consequences can short-circuit a couple's sex life.

When Lee Anders carried his bride, Cheryl, across the threshold, he was a virgin and she wasn't.

"I never knew love before I became a Christian and met my husband—all I knew was sex," said Cheryl. "Plus, I'd never experienced any sexual gratification from the boys I was with in high school. At the time I didn't think there would be consequences later on. But I was wrong."

Lee agreed. "Her sexual promiscuity definitely impacted our day-to-day communication about sex."

Sexually, all the plumbing worked for the Anders, but deep doubts clouded their minds. *I wonder if she's comparing me to those other guys,* Lee thought. *She probably thinks I'm a sexual geek.*

Cheryl wondered, *Should I tell Lee he should be doing this before he does that?* In addition, she was often racked with guilt each time they rumbled under the sheets—which greatly affected her sexual desire. But she kept quiet, and their lovemaking became more and more infrequent.

It took ten years before the couple was able to face the music—typical for the Dark Ages. The Anders stood at opposite ends of the sexual desire scale. But after finally concluding they needed to find a middle ground, they sought the Lord *together* on the frequency issue. That's when they came out of the Dark Ages in this area.

Said Lee, "You can read books, make charts, and fill out questionnaires, but the bottom line was how well we were taking our problem to Jesus Christ. That's not a trite statement! Once we did that, all the other issues fell into place, including our sexual expectations."

Lee also says he's learned that it's OK to experience times of unrequited love. "If my marital satisfaction is dependent on how many times we have sex, then I'm going to be walking around with a droopy face. My priority should be on having a godly marriage and being the best husband I can be. I've found that's all dependent on my attitude . . . which is dependent on my relationship with God."

What We Learned

Those who jumped God's gun and were sexually active before marriage have been forgiven by God—if repentance has occurred. Once they've been forgiven, it is as though they never sinned in God's eyes. The Lord tells us in Isaiah 43:25 that "I, even I, am he who blots out your transgressions, for my own sake, and remembers your sins no more."

If you've never truly repented, can you take a moment to confess your sin and ask God for his forgiveness? He's waiting to hear from you. Christ is capable of throwing your sins into the deepest sea, although the *consequences* of sins can remain on the surface for years, as this second-decade husband notes.

"I know our sex life would be better if I had waited," Jerry told us. "I strayed beyond God's boundary, and because of that, those long-ago sins have affected today's sexual relations. For instance, I'll resent it if she doesn't want to do a certain position, when my old girlfriend and I always made love that way. She also has different ideas about foreplay than my past flames. Having premarital sex has been the biggest regret of my life, and it has taken me years to put the past behind me. Repentance pointed to the road to recovery."

Can She Trust Your Love?

We can't imagine why, but women often don't trust a man's motives. Strange, huh? The way a man pursues affection from his wife is often the determining factor of when their sex life will get out of the Dark Ages.

"The first twelve years of marriage," Mack Porter admits, "I was as selfish as a man could be. My wife had her faults, but she wasn't anywhere near my level. The last five we've had a whole new relationship. We've both grown up.

"For me, I've learned not to demand anything. Though wanting sex is obviously OK, if an evening or weekend doesn't end in sex, I can still move toward her in love. If I'm manipulating her, she knows I'm not loving her.

"I've had to ponder *what it means to love Jackie no matter how she responds to me.* If I retreat when there's rejection or when I manipulate situations in a blatant way to get what I think I need, am I really showing love?"

Mack has also perceptively asked himself the question, *What expression would my love for her take if I were to pursue her at levels I've never done before?*

"I finally realized that my wife is a responder. She's built to respond to biblical masculinity and genuine love.

"The men I've met with over the years gravitate to things that make them feel competent: work, hobbies, sports, even masturbation. That last one is something you can't fail at. You can enter into a fantasy world where you have power; and every woman is seduced. With my wife, however, I feel like we're guaranteed to be incompetent. We know we can't do this relationship thing perfectly."

What We Learned

Depending on how long selfishness has been the norm in a marriage, it may take a year or more of a man loving his wife unconditionally for her to really trust him. Wives will be suspicious, but if they were asked what they really wanted most from their husbands, love with pure motives would be among the top three on their list. As Mack pointed out, "It takes a tremendous amount of strength and courage to move toward our wives in genuine love when there is absolutely no guarantee of success. Yet that's the key. I think women are dying for men to risk something other than sexual advances. Although they may reject a man's first attempts at changing his approach, they're saying, 'Please don't stop being nice.'"

TOP TEN REASONS WHY SEX IS BETTER IN THE SECOND DECADE

10. With the kids out of the house more often, you can see what she looks like during daylight.

9. Your bodies have more "give."

8. The late-evening electric shave has become a habit.

7. You're not too proud to admit to being exhausted three-quarters of the way through.

6. By the second decade, hubby has learned that there are better ways to set the mood for intimacy than begging, pouting, and negotiating.

5. You've finally saved up enough dough to move out of your parents' house.

4. You're finally used to her never taking her socks off.

3. There are *finally* a couple dozen Christian books on sex.

2. Beginner's luck is no longer a factor.

1. You're hoping anything has to be better than the first decade.

A Six-Month Dry Spell

Though Aaron and Anita Flemming married young (before age twenty), they lived an idyllic first decade of love. They ate out regularly, traveled to foreign countries, purchased their dream home, . . . and became the happiest parents on earth when Anita announced she was expecting. Could life get any better than this?

"I had a terrible pregnancy," Anita says. "I expected Aaron

to be Mr. Affectionate, like he had been our first nine years, but he wasn't very sympathetic to my morning sickness or waves of nausea. He never did the little things I thought he should do. I began to lose respect for him."

When Caitlin was born, Aaron thought life would return to normal—which meant twice-or-thrice-a-week sexual relations. *Hey, I've been a patient guy these last few months,* he thought. *Besides, how could she forget how great we had it before Caitlin was born?*

When Aaron began to voice his thoughts, all Anita heard was the ramblings of an inconsiderate, sex-crazed man. *Doesn't he understand my feelings? Whenever he brings home flowers or tries to be extra nice, I can see right through him. He wants sex.*

Anita was right, and the situation didn't improve much after daughter number two was born.

One evening Anita finally worked up the nerve to talk to him. "How do I know you love me for me and not for sex?" she asked. "I just can't jump in the sack with you every time you get that look in your eye."

The situation deteriorated so much that the Flemmings sought a counselor. After several sessions, Aaron agreed to wait until she was ready. Guess what? They waited for *six months!*

"We needed to go out and eat at a nice restaurant without the expectation that sex would top off the evening," Aaron says. "That happened on several occasions over six months. The night we resumed our sexual relations, we had gone out and had a nice evening together. We came home, and she initiated sex. That was great, because she saw I was willing to wait as long as it took. I wanted *her* to want *me.*"

What We Learned

Counseling proved to be the Reformation Aaron and Anita needed to move their sex life out of the Dark Ages. Several other couples told us they weren't too proud to seek help when their relationship took a U-turn after kids arrived. All of them said it was the best thing they could have done.

Worthwhile Advice

Many couples we talked to wished someone had told them what to expect during the various stages of their sexual relationship. Here are a few roadblocks couples may face in the second decade of love:

Dilemma: After children, sexual frequency will decrease—count on it! Mom subtly shifts her focus to the child, and even when she comes around to romance, she's usually too pooped to work up much interest.

Why is she tired? She's getting up in the middle of the night to calm a crying baby, waking up early for breast feedings, packing up half the house to go anywhere, running the child to the doctor, and trying to keep ahead of the laundry piles. Even if your kids are beyond the infant stage, Mom still has a lot of responsibilities to them. Meanwhile, Dad is wondering what happened to those impromptu trysts on Saturday morning.

Answer: Men, deal with it! We know you don't want to hear those harsh words, but place yourself in your wife's slippers. Backing off on sex is one way to serve your wife during this trying time. Probably, sex will have to be planned, which isn't too bad, because planning it gives women a couple of days to *think* about it. That helps keep intimacy . . . intimate.

Wives, if you don't have the energy for romantic, passionate love like the B.C. (Before Children) days, that's OK. There will be times when you'll just be meeting his sexual needs. Try not to lay a guilt trip on him for initiating, asking, begging, or whatever (men's egos bruise easily here). Once in a blue moon, *you* can initiate sex.

Many couples reported having a "sexual renaissance" after the early years of meeting *every* need for their child had passed. "Now that our kids are older," an Oregon woman told us, "I'm feeling the freedom to start things going. I've even bought sexy, black lingerie! We know sex is important, so we've both really made an effort to give it the place it deserves."

Dilemma: They did everything "but" before they got married.

Answer: Rodger and Rita Kaiser were young Christians before they married, but they were singed when they got too close to the flame of passion. They were not alone. Sex researchers Dr. Samuel S. Janus and his wife, Dr. Cynthia L. Janus, reported in their book *The Janus Report on Sexual Behavior* that 50 percent of religious people said they had "very much or much" sexual experience before marriage. This sample includes those who remained "technical virgins."

"We petted heavily before marriage," said Rita, "and we knew it was wrong. Sin is sin, and it did leave scars. Now I can see why Dr. Dobson says girls will give sex to get love, and boys will tell girls they love them to get sex. I think I gave up something very precious to receive love and affection."

Rita felt she had been cornered by Rodger. "He was

putting the moves on me. I didn't have good enough self-esteem to say no. Shortly afterward, we decided to get married, but we had to deal with the consequences of our actions on our honeymoon. Not being completely new to each other was a big one. There was a sense that, yes, we've done this before. We both knew very clearly what we had done was wrong. Although the green light was on after we married, we wondered, *Is this really OK?*"

The guilt stayed with Rita until her tenth year of marriage when she dealt with her sin before God and tearfully told her husband how much he had hurt her years ago. "He was so sorry about it," said Rita. "He cried, too, and I was able to forgive him, as Christ forgave me."

Dilemma: A Nevada man said that while he was growing up his family never talked about sex, religion, or politics.

Answer: If you grew up in a home where sex was never discussed (and many couples did), then there'll be a lot of skirting this issue. Recognize what's happening as early as possible. Fight the urge to keep quiet. During the second decade of love, there is simply too much potential for long-term conflict if expectations go unspoken or needs go unmet.

Dilemma: Some husbands and wives grew up with little or no affection, so they find it difficult to initiate romance. Not so for Jill. She told us that her sex life was great because she was affectionate by nature. "My whole family is like that. But I have girlfriends who believe sex is a chore."

Answer: We're not suggesting couples need to take personality tests to determine what level of affection a spouse has to move up to. But we did hear—often—that the level of affection they received from their parents played a big part in their ability to be affectionate with their husbands. These issues usually didn't surface until the later part of the first decade of marriage. That's when couples settled into patterns they were comfortable with.

Though the melody is different, the words are the same: communicate, communicate, communicate!

"From a female standpoint, the sexual relationship *is* communication," said Diana Seymour. "For the first ten years of our marriage, our sex life stunk because of poor communication . . . about almost everything. I was definitely not an open person to my husband. Partly because I was raising four kids, I was tired, and sex was always an effort. If we'd had good communication, that area of our lives would have been different."

Dilemma: How to get out of the same old rut during the second decade of love.

Answer: Cindy Clark, married twenty years, loves to camp and sleep outdoors. In fact, she feels particularly amorous under an indigo blanket of stars. The trouble is, they don't go camping very much, so her husband, Dave, did the next best thing: He put up some sheets of plywood around their outdoor deck, and two or three times a month during the summer, the Clarks roll out their sleeping bags and spend the night outside. "It's terribly romantic," said Dave. "Unless we've had sex recently, it will happen, because I see it catering to Cindy's idea of romance, what with all the stars above our heads."

Dilemma: He wishes his wife was a Christian nymphomaniac.

Answer: One of our funny stories in *"Daddy's Home"* came

from Jay, who told us his goal in life was to marry a godly Marilyn Monroe. He didn't marry a sexpot, but Donna is a very attractive woman. However, she's not the pin-up type—nor does she seek that role.

During their first decade of love, Jay thought he'd move things along by buying his wife a sexy negligee—one of those see-through jobs you find in Frederick's of Hollywood. When Donna opened the box and held up the skimpy teddy, she thought it was some kind of joke. When she realized he was serious, she nearly beat him over the head with the box.

Recently, I called Jay and Donna again to talk about the black negligee story. "That was probably the major crisis in our marriage when I bought that nightgown," said Jay. "What I did was purchase something in black lace for someone who is used to pink flannel. I wasn't accepting her for who she was. I was not cherishing my wife."

Their story has a happy ending. During the middle of the second decade of love, Jay and Donna went out to dinner on Valentine's Day. After dessert Donna handed Jay a wrapped box. "Here's your present," she said.

Inside were three satin nighties—in pink, white, and beige. A note said, "I will model these for you after dinner."

Donna chuckled at the memory. "I wish I had a camera at dinner," she said. "Jay was absolutely speechless."

Dilemma: During the second decade of love, the kids are young teenagers. What do we do now?

Answer: A lot of parents told us their teens stayed up later than they did, which cramped their style. The walls can be very thin, especially if teens are across the hall.

"We feel like there must be an arousal alarm in our teens' bedrooms," said Stephanie Jones, married sixteen years. "They always seem to come in to talk to us at the funniest times. It can get on your nerves. It's not easy squeezing in a sex life in addition to everything else going on in our lives."

Having a sense of humor has helped. Sometimes Stephanie and Bud Jones will flirt outrageously in the supermarket, and in the old days, they would rush home, jump into bed, and finish the thing off. But now, with older kids staring at them, they wonder what the teens are thinking. That can be inhibiting.

What the Joneses have done is make sex *exciting*. "Sometimes when the house is empty, I'll say, 'Quick, the kids are gone for an hour,' and that keeps sex on a fresh level for us," said Stephanie.

We bet it does!

The Ultimate Endurance Test

When Bill and Maggie Strothers married in their midtwenties, neither could have suspected what lay ahead. During the first year of matrimony, the Strotherses' sex life was "vigorous" (in other words, almost every day). When child number one came along three years later, things had naturally tapered off. But after child number two, their sex life ground to a screeching halt.

"I became what you call 'frigid,'" says Maggie.

Oh really? How long did that last? Three or four months?

"For fourteen years I rarely had any interest in sex. Our lovemaking during that time was very sporadic."

Yikes! Fourteen years! How could that have happened? Was

Bill a total jerk or something? Was he abusive? Didn't he ever help out in the kitchen or get the kids bathed and into bed?

"There was nothing wrong with Bill. We didn't know it at the time, but it likely stemmed back to unresolved issues with my father. I don't remember my father sexually abusing me, but I had all the classic symptoms."

Bill says his father-in-law wasn't a very nice guy, but Maggie was loyal until the end. "Just before he died, Maggie and her father expressed their love for each other," explained Bill. "But when he was gone, it was like a supernatural evil was broken. We were able to resume normal sexual relations shortly after his death five years ago."

But what went through Maggie's mind during those fourteen years? How did Bill survive?

"We worked at communication," Maggie says. "Twice we spent weeks talking with counselors just to get a third person's opinion. We read every book. We attended every conference. But nothing helped us turn the corner sexually."

Looking back, Maggie says it was incredible that Bill stuck with her during those long periods of rejection. "I know there were occasions when he wanted to walk out of the marriage and find another wife. We'd talk about what to do, but I was paralyzed and unable to respond. I cried and felt extremely inadequate. Bill, for the most part, did his best. He affirmed me in other areas so I wouldn't feel like a total failure. What lifted my spirits was when he'd say, 'I realize you're not intentionally doing this.'"

Nice job, Bill. But what was going through your mind? You had to have been one frustrated dude.

"During the first seven years of her frigidity, I thought

counseling was the answer. The therapists focused on communication, believing if that improved, sex would follow. But even Maggie admitted that better communication wouldn't solve her problem. She just had an unexplainable revulsion toward physical contact."

Maggie avoided any long hugs or deep kisses for fear that it might lead to sex, even if they were standing in the kitchen in the middle of a Saturday afternoon. Bill could sneak a quick peck, but she was afraid anything more would start his motors.

One evening after a counseling appointment (right around the seven-year mark), Bill remembers the two of them agreeing to this: "Whether we ever fix this or not, we still love each other, and we're going to continue to love each other. We're not going to let this ruin a wonderful marriage."

For her part, Maggie told Bill that when he wanted to make love, they'd make love. And Bill agreed she didn't have to pretend she was enjoying it. She told Bill just to let her know when he was ready, and she wouldn't reject him. That helped Bill meet his immediate need for sexual release. Although their lovemaking was perfunctory, they knew this arrangement would keep their marriage intact.

The long winter without much sex did have one positive aspect. "We picked up some great communication skills," said Bill. "A marriage encounter weekend taught us to express positive and negative emotions in 'neutral.' We began to set aside ten minutes a day to talk after dinner. We'd leave the dishes on the table, go over to the couch, and I'd rub her feet while we talked. The communication flowed."

After their sexual relationship was rekindled, Maggie says the last five years have been a gift from the Lord—"but we still haven't *totally* recovered," she said. "Sometimes Bill holds back for fear of rejection. That's when I remind him that he has the freedom to initiate sex whenever he wants to."

What We Learned

Guys: Do you think times are tough when a month slips by and there's no sex? Ponder the plight of poor Bill, who came up empty-handed for months at a stretch. Yet Bill didn't die (although he probably learned to appreciate cold showers). His story underscores the idea that sex is a drive, not a need. We have *needs* for air and food that must be satisfied. Sex is a *drive* that must be channeled. That means we can control it with our mind and will.

Let us paint a word picture. Let's say Bill and Maggie have two cars in the garage. One is a '56 Corvette they take out on dates to park and well, you know, do all that lovey-dovey stuff. Early in their marriage, the couple drove the roadster several times a week. But suddenly, Maggie told Bill to leave the hot rod in the garage. She wasn't interested in "parking" with her husband.

Meanwhile, their other car, a family station wagon, represents the more mundane aspects of marriage and child rearing. For fourteen years, the wagon racked up a lot of miles—but few trips to Lover's Lane. Bill may have thought he was justified to take out his cherry red sports car by himself and find female companionship. But he remembered his vow to love and cherish Maggie "for better or worse." In the end God honored his patience and restored their sexual relationship, and Bill once again romanced Maggie in their Little Deuce Coupe.

A Closing Thought

We want to end this chapter with the inspirational story of Billy and Brenda Adams. When the Adamses were engaged over eleven years ago, friends took Billy aside. "You should know that not all sexual encounters will be a ten, with romantic music playing in the background," one friend quipped.

Billy and Brenda, in their midtwenties, had been saving themselves for each other. As virgins, however, they did not want to be unprepared for the start of their sexual relationship, so they read Kevin Leman's *Sex Begins in the Kitchen* and Cliff and Joyce Penner's *The Gift of Sex* on the couch together. (Now *that* took willpower . . . talking about sex and intimacy but not doing anything about it.)

"One of the last chapters in Leman's book is 'Ying, Yang,' which lists all the slang terms for the penis," said Brenda. "We just cracked up reading that stuff. But what it did was get us verbal about what so many people are afraid to mention: body parts."

Nonetheless, at their last premarital counseling session, their pastor imparted this advice: "Don't expect a lot of fireworks on your honeymoon night."

OK, we'll buy that, they thought.

Still, the young couple was pretty excited. After the wedding, the long reception, and the drive to their honeymoon hideaway, the big moment had arrived. Brenda unpacked two nightgowns and held them up. "Which one should I wear?" she asked her new husband.

When Billy pointed at the pink lace chiffon, Brenda slipped into the bathroom. When she came out into the darkened room, she suddenly realized all the boundaries were gone. All the waiting was over . . . and she felt sick to her stomach.

She scooted under the covers, but her nerves shot to the ceiling. "Honey, I think I'm going to throw up," she said, covering her mouth. She ran to the bathroom.

When she returned, Brenda was still as white as the bed sheets. She sat on the bed and moaned. Billy drew near and put his arms around her. "Sweetie, we can just go to sleep. We don't have to have sex tonight."

Can you believe it? Neither could Brenda.

"Let me tell you what it did for me," she said. "It instilled confidence that he loved me. Here we were, legally married, and he had all these rights, but he laid down those rights—all for my benefit. When I awoke the next morning, I felt complete security *[mark that word]* over how much he cared for *me* and not my body. Believe me, I woke up raring to go. Billy was a bit surprised, though pleasantly. Afterward, we took a bath together, and I thought it would be a long time before I could do something like *that* with him. I really believe his sensitivity and gentleness on our wedding night had a lot to do with instilling a great sexual confidence in me."

What We Learned

Men, our honeymoons are long gone, but can we still lay down our so-called rights? Can we take a step back and realize that not demanding sex tonight may be the most loving thing we can do? Keep that in mind the next time you have "that look in your eye."

GEMS TO THINK ON

- "The extent of my premarital knowledge about sex was watching a junior-high movie, *Little Girls Grow Up*. My mom never gave me any information—until the night before I got married. She came into my room with that look on her face, and I thought, *Oh no, you've got to be kidding*. She said there were two things I ought to know: That the morning after my wedding night I would be so ashamed that I couldn't look myself in the mirror; and two, she had heard that Italians were rough."

- "If we have an intimate conversation, I tell her we don't have to have sex. That lets her know every close feeling we have for each other doesn't have to be consummated."

- "I can't go from putting kids down to jumping into bed with my husband. If I nurse before bedtime, and then when I retire my husband has an interest in the breast area, it's hard to feel like a sex goddess. There are a lot of emotional hurdles a young mom must take before she can get to the bedroom. I don't think men can really relate to that."

- "After twelve years of marriage, we learned to separate lovemaking from other agendas. That means we no longer withhold sex to punish the other, nor use it as a Band-Aid to gloss over big issues."

- "We've been married thirty years, and these days the pinnacle isn't the sex act—our friendship is. Emotional highs are far more meaningful than sexual highs these days."

- "To help us keep the romance alive, we eat by candle-light every evening, except during the summertime. Even when the children were growing up, we just turned out the lights and lit the candles. They loved it."

- "Sex means two different things to a man and a woman. To the man it's *immediate* gratification. To the woman it's *gradual* gratification. My wife and I are built for each other like a lock and key. But a lock is not a key. What she needs is different from what I need in terms of intensity and frequency. In our eighteen years of marriage, our needs have changed over time as the relationship grew."

- "We read all the books about sexual response, and we decided that although the national average for frequency may be 3.2 times a week, we were going to have sex when we wanted to have sex."

- "Sex is best when we take time to romance. That means we think about each other throughout the day and look forward to being together. My husband calls home often. When he's around, he holds me a lot. That may or may not lead to sex . . . but it certainly leads to affection."

- "Sexually, men are greedy. Most guys never think they get enough."

- "Just as women have a cycle, so do men. About ten years into our marriage, I discussed my sexual cycle with my wife. She trusted me enough to realize I wasn't just trying to up the frequency count. That finally turned things around for us. She understood that men are different from women. And she also realized she hadn't married this incredible pervert!"

- "There are nights when I'm scheming up ways to get her ready for me, even though I *know* she's not emotionally willing to give. To be honest, I've been quite unreasonable. The Renaissance we want to attain sexually is to learn how to value each other the way God wants us to."

- "If both husband and wife will communicate about needs, expectations, and what they like, then their

sex lives will be a joy. If they don't communicate . . .
ugh!"

♦ "We have friends who will take our kids for a few hours
just so we can spend time together. We do the same for
them. That's been one of the best arrangements we've
made."

♦ "We once read a book that talked about orgasms. I was
uncomfortable discussing such a subject, but it was
important for my husband to tell me about the
intimacies of sex."

♦ "What message do you send your wife after sex? Do
you ignore her? Stop caressing her? If you do, then
all you wanted was the action. Continue to whisper
to her. Don't roll over and fall asleep. You will
communicate more in the first few moments *after* sex,
because at that point she is so attentive to her husband.
I've told guys that, and they look dumbfounded. They
didn't have a clue that they were giving their wife two
messages: One is love, and the other is 'Thanks, now
I'm outta here.'"

♦ "We've been married twenty years, and the last eight
years have been the best. Our maturity level means we
can communicate a whole lot better. Before then, the
extent of our communication was, 'Is tonight the night?'
Now we can joke about it, and we both enjoy it as never
before."

YOU KNEW THIS WOULD TOP THE LIST

What do we like to do the best? Researchers for the
Americans' Use of Time Project surveyed 2,500 adults and
asked them to rank 200 ordinary activities on a scale of
1 to 10.

Nearest to a perfect 10 was sex, with a rating of 9.3,
closely followed by playing sports (9.2) and, believe it or not,

fishing (9.1). Hugging and kissing was rated an 8.8, the same as playing with kids.

What do we *least* like to do? Visiting the dentist (4.7) and taking the car to a repair shop (4.6).

Fragile:
Handle with Care

W ho I am (circa 1944):

- "I'm a farmer. I work my eighty acres fourteen hours a day."

- "I'm a factory worker. I build fuselages for Hughes Aircraft."

- "I'm a mother. I keep a house running smoothly and raise six children."

- "I'm a youngster. I feed the chickens before breakfast, and after school I help Dad with chores until sundown."

- "I'm a Christian. I go to church every Sunday. I don't cuss, dance, or listen to Frank Sinatra on the radio."

Who I am (circa 1994):

- "I'm a young professional. It took six years and $120,000 to earn my MBA at Stanford, but my degree landed me a good job with a Detroit firm. My love life? I recently met my significant other at a Young Turks mixer. We don't have time for each other during the week, but on weekends we party hearty."

- "I'm a single mom. My ex left me because he got tired of the commitment. The kids have adjusted to him not being around. He wasn't a good example anyway. I'd love to get married again, but most men I meet are scuzzballs. Besides, as soon as they find out I've got three kids, they're history."

- "I'm a teenage girl. If I don't wear the right clothes and go out with the right guys, I can kiss popularity goodbye. I can't wait to get out of high school. Then I can get out from under my mom's thumb, wear my hair the way I want, stay out as late as I want, and start having some real fun."

- "I'm a working mother. My kids are in grade school, but a nearby day care picks them up and watches them until 5:30. It costs a lot to live in a neighborhood with a good school district, but my husband and I are willing to make the sacrifice. I'm making twenty-seven thousand dollars a year."

- "I'm a busy dad. I'm on the road every morning at 6:00 A.M.; any later, and my seventy-mile commute becomes a living nightmare. The return trip takes longer. I usually pull into the driveway around 7:15. My goal in life? Eight hours of uninterrupted shut-eye. Sunday's the only day I can sleep in. We used to go to church

early in our marriage, but after the kids arrived,
by the wayside."

See yourself in any of those snapshots? Maybe, maybe
not, but either way you probably know someone who does.
We share these vignettes with you to illustrate a point: Life
is a lot more complicated today. Just fifty years ago, most
everyone understood what their roles were. You worked
because no one worked *for* you; the government's safety net
wasn't very big. You stayed married because divorce was a
scandal—something neighbors gossiped about on party
lines. You stayed home and tried to raise well-adjusted
children, although you sensed an uncertain world beyond
your picket fence. You went to church because your faithful
parents taught you to be faithful kids.

In the late 1940s author Aldous Huxley predicted in *Brave
New World* that parenthood would give way to test-tube babies
and state-run nurseries. That hasn't panned out, although
today we *can* create human beings in a petri dish. Huxley failed
to foresee that the state couldn't smother human emotions
such as love, tenderness, compassion—even insecurity.

A generation later our society can point to tremendous
advances in knowledge. The "information superhighway" is
a new thoroughfare with tremendous implications. Before
this decade is out, parents will be able to turn on a computer
modem and hook up with a James Dobson network, for
instance. (Maybe you'll be able to interact with us. Wouldn't
that be a hoot!) Got a problem with marital communication? Log in. Is your hubby failing to back you up in front
of the kids? Advice is just seconds away.

We say all this to make a point: All the Intel chips and fiber-optic relays in the world won't change human nature. God included egos and all the subsequent human foibles when he breathed life into our souls. We are fragile people, and when two of those egos are combined in the pressure cooker of marriage, insecurities can arise. If we've been wronged, we want someone to pay. In marriage it's usually the spouse who gets handed the bill. It's been that way ever since Adam tried to blame Eve for passing him the forbidden fruit.

This is how we addressed insecurity in our interviews:

> *Question 19: Husbands and wives have areas they are insecure in. How do you try to build up your spouse's weak area instead of using it as a weapon?*

Just like the inquiries about sex, this question opened up a Pandora's box. Prior to our interviews, we predicted men would have more to say about their wives' insecurity than vice versa. We were right. Though men are insecure, their wives didn't have much to say. Usually, a man's insecurity is work related. If the job is going well, we're happy guys. If we're laid off, we're shattered.

Women, however, are more sensitive to the voices whispering they don't measure up—whether it's at home or in the workplace. Women struggle in this area, mainly because society is sending them mixed messages about what their roles should be. (A typical one: "Who wants to stay home in the company of toddlers with dirty diapers? Only a career can give a woman fulfillment.")

We are going to zero in on several of these insecurity

issues, and we will deal with them in a "one, two, three" fashion using these questions:

- ◆ 1. What is the insecurity?

- ◆ 2. How did it get there?

- ◆ 3. What can husbands do to build their wives up instead of using the insecurity as a weapon to gain more control? And what can the wife do herself to help counteract the false messages the world is sending her?

This short, practical approach won't solve deep-seated problems of self-image, but it will help spouses understand why their counterparts don't feel good about themselves.

"What Did I Inherit?"

We wish we could say that most of the men we spoke with married secure, emotionally stable women . . . but we can't. Some women admitted bringing to the marriage counter enough emotional baggage for two persons. At the end of the honeymoon, the new husband even had to pick up some extra luggage at the airport carousel.

"When I married Angie," Tray Smith told us, "she had some deep insecurities I didn't know existed. I thought I was marrying a together, healthy person."

Surprise! As the insecurities manifested themselves in the early years of marriage, Tray wasn't much help. "The stuff her father programmed into her—'you're a dumb blonde'—was unwittingly continued by me, too. Along with everyone else, I laughed at her father's little jokes. Without realizing it, I figured she wasn't very smart. For instance, if I wanted to talk about spiritual issues, I never bothered to bring them up with her. I thought she wasn't up to the task. My attitude reinforced her feelings of unworthiness that she couldn't communicate about deep things. When we went out to social gatherings, I sought out like-minded people for stimulating conversations and left her to talk with the women about the kids. She felt increasingly insecure.

"About five years into the marriage, however, I began to discover that she did have a mind, and it was a good one. We began to talk about the work we were doing in the church together, and she impressed me with some of her insights. As I sought more input, she became more confident about herself."

Tray noticed something else after several years of marriage. When Angie's father was around, she would crawl back into her shell of inferiority. "That just tells me how badly *we* can mess our kids up if we're not careful," said Tray.

Now that their children are older, Angie recently went back to college and learned something important: She's just as smart as today's students! She is earning A's and finding her name on the dean's list.

One, Two, Three

1. The insecurity: feelings of worthlessness
2. How it got there: a father who never built up the self-esteem of his daughter and a young husband who reinforced the idea that she didn't measure up
3. What to do—husband: Look for feelings of insecurity in

your first decade of marriage. If you can recognize the warning signals early on, you won't reinforce a parent's lies. Instead, bring her into your circle and heap on the praise.

What to do—wife: Recognize that you've been told things that aren't true. Ask yourself: What do I do well? Where can I use those skills? How can I turn my weaknesses into strengths?

The Other Men

It may be hard to understand that before you walked into her life and swept her away, your wife might have dated some real jerks. Or, if yours is a remarriage, the ex really did a number on her.

Past relationships can play a big role in how women view themselves, as well as affecting their attitudes about men. Some males, in an effort to control women, make their mates feel "lower than a snake's belly in a wagon rut" (as Jed Clampett of the *Beverly Hillbillies* used to say). Then you have situations where her former boyfriends based their affection on her appearance or whether she did or *didn't* put out.

Hal Lyons told us his wife, Debbie, was repeatedly wooed and then dumped by guys who wanted more than she was willing to give. Guys were after one thing, and it wasn't her help on their algebra homework.

After they got married, Debbie willingly gave of herself, but once that sexual mountain had been conquered, their relationship hit the skids. Why? Debbie thought Hal would soon be scouting the horizons for someone else. Isn't sex all guys are interested in? Her insecurity led to jealousy.

Hal recognized what was happening, and he took steps to reassure his wife that she was the only one for him. "I always sought to be extra-businesslike when I was in the company of other women," said Hal. "I even put myself under unreasonable restraints. But that's part of dealing with your wife's weakness. It's recognizing where the other person is vulnerable and then protecting her from it."

One, Two, Three

1. The insecurity: wondering if her husband would stray into extramarital affairs
2. How it got there: Before the marriage old boyfriends wanted to get physical.
3. What to do—husband: Stay on the up-and-up. Be patient until she says it's no longer a problem. Protecting her from insecurity means you *never* use it as a weapon to hurt her.

    What to do—wife: Don't blame your husband for insecurities he didn't create. Acknowledge or reward his efforts to show grace.

Never a Kind Word

What happens when children grow up without hearing words of encouragement or a warm compliment?

Janet Nellis was the youngest of six children in a household where both parents worked outside the home. "It seems as though the only attention I got was when my dad called me a runt," she said. "I excelled in several areas, yet my mother never complimented me for anything. Although they were loving parents, they forgot to do the little things that make kids feel special."

What has her husband done to counterbalance those years of inattention?

"We're nearly fifty years old, and my husband, Jay, has spent our entire marriage complimenting me."

Still, after nearly three decades of marriage, Janet has a hard time accepting a compliment. "Even though I've been a consistent encourager," Jay says, "she still can't bring herself to feel worthy of praise. I was raised by parents who always told me I was a unique creation of God, that I could do anything if I just tried. That's encouragement. I believe God put us together because he was aware Janet needed someone to lift her up."

One, Two, Three

1. The insecurity: not having truly internalized the truth about who she is as God's unique creation
2. How it got there: Both parents, but especially Mom, never reinforced that truth. Plus, Mom never complimented her daughter no matter what she excelled in.
3. What to do—husband: Point her to the Scripture passages that describe our worth in God's eyes. Encourage her every chance you get. Insecurities formed by years of neglect often take years to fix.

    What to do—wife: Let the Bible—God's Word—speak directly to you. Then believe what it says!

God Is the Answer

When something is lacking from her early years, it's tempting for a woman to look to her husband for everything. But he can only do so much. There must come a time when a wife realizes that (a) God is capable of doing more for her than her husband could ever do, and (b) the strength that God can provide lasts longer.

As a young wife, Laurie Simpson remembers leading a Bible study for single women. "I was teaching these women that God was the only one who could meet their real needs; that a man wasn't the missing piece to their lives. Suddenly, I realized that I wasn't practicing that principle in my own life.

"My husband, Robert, is an extremely capable man. Unknowingly, I was putting too much pressure on him to be Mr. Ideal for everything. I wanted him to build me up in areas where I was lacking."

Not all men feel good about themselves, either. Although only a couple of women we interviewed mentioned that their husbands had a poor self-concept, we know men's insecurities can run deep, too.

Carol Hammond said that when their marriage hit a crisis point, this was one area she zeroed in on.

"I was always trying to build Chris up," she says. "I'd tell him that he was a great person to be around. I always complimented him for the things he did around the house. But when our problems started, I told him I'd been trying to build his self-image for years, but now I was sick of it. The compliments I had given him were true, but he was finally going to have to stand on his own two feet and allow God to build him up. I couldn't make him like himself."

Chris remembers thinking through Carol's words for a long minute. "Yeah, maybe you're right," he said, not wanting to lose face and concede. But as time passed, Chris began sticking up for himself when home-front confrontation hit. He doesn't back down anymore.

One, Two, Three

1. The insecurity: needing the spouse to "complete" his or her life
2. How it got there: It could have been family, church, or other outside influences. If you think about it, years of watching Disney family movies can do it for any girl. They reinforce the idea that a girl can't be happy until she's married to Prince Charming.
3. What to do—spouse who's trying to meet every need: Your spouse will find out sooner or later that you can't do it, so make it sooner. Before the stagecoach turns back into a pumpkin, remind him or her that God didn't bring you together so you could meet *all* of each other's needs. Yes, you'll do what you can to shore up areas that are lacking, but ultimately, God can do more than you can.

    What to do—spouse who expects all your needs to be met: Examine your expectations. Are you unconsciously ascribing a role to your spouse that only God can play? If so, realize that he or she can only do so much to build you up and that God's handiwork is much more complete.

Projecting Insecurity

You see it on every grade school playground: children constantly putting their classmates down. Why? Some kids feel better about themselves after delivering a well-timed verbal blow. Most children outgrow this behavior, but some don't.

Not only did Cathy Lowery catch it in the school yard,

but her parents relied on put-downs to maintain discipline. No matter how well she did at school, her parents could find one small area of fault.

"My parents were the type to find something bad, even in the excellent report cards I brought home. Consequently, I have tended to look for chinks in the armor of my husband, Wes. When I talk to him negatively, he'll usually ask me if that's really what I mean. Or he'll say, 'That hurt.' That's his way of helping me. His honesty is sometimes irritating—even after thirty years of him trying to help me look at things in a more positive light."

One, Two, Three

1. The insecurity: needing to tear someone else down to feel better about yourself
2. How it got there: a parent who continuously found fault instead of commenting on the good
3. What to do—spouse on the receiving end: Don't trade insult for insult. Ask your spouse to clarify the real intent of the remark. Calmly state that the comment stung. Be patient as your spouse learns how to communicate.

   What to do—spouse giving the put-down: You can live by this age-old advice I (Mike) constantly heard from my mom: "If you don't have something nice to say, then it's not worth saying."

Back to School

Husbands, are you a student of your wife's menstrual cycle? Instead of being patient and understanding, we're often uncaring and insensitive. At a time when she's feeling low, we revert to teenage machismo:

- ♦ "Hey, is it your time of the month?"

- ♦ "When you're going through your female time, just tell me so I can stay away."

- ♦ "Honey, for twenty-five days you're wonderful, but the other five . . . it's like night and day."

Those statements are sure to boost her self-worth, right guys?
The best place to look for help is found in 1 Peter 3:7. The KJV translation says that husbands should live with their wives according to "knowledge." That means we need to go to school on our wives: Study them; know their ups and downs.

"Guys don't have a clue" was one comment we heard. *Yeah, from a woman, right?* Wrong! This came from Jay Williams, a counselor who has spent hundreds of hours unraveling the root causes of marital conflict.

"Men live with their wife for decades and don't have any idea what's going on in her body," Jay claims. "All they know is she's irritable four or five days each month. Hundreds of times I've had couples come in for counseling after a big fight. One of the first questions I ask the wife is, 'Where were you in your monthly cycle?' Naturally, women are hostile to that question. But I persist until I get an answer. In nearly all instances, the fight occurred in the few days leading up to the woman's period. Then I turn to the husband and say, 'Did you understand she was experiencing premenstrual tension? Do you know what that is?' Very few husbands are in the know."

In the past few years, I (Mike) have kept track. I don't do this to receive a pat on my back but out of self-defense. Invariably, our big fights, our stinging comments, our bullheaded disagreements have happened during Nicole's premenstrual period. I've learned the hard way, and so has Nicole. Now, she'll tell me she's experiencing PMS. Knowing that bit of information has helped us get through some rocky moments.

Counselor Jay Williams says most men aren't tracking their wife's menstrual cycle, so when the PMS blowups occur, the husband's reaction is to pour fuel on the fire, to match emotion for emotion. "I've seen many husbands bait and inflame their wives' emotional weaknesses," said Jay. "What a husband needs to do is be aware of his wife's calendar. If he can be sensitive for several days a month, the emotional trauma can be minimized."

One, Two, Three

1. The insecurity: The woman feels fat, grouchy, and irritable. She probably harbors another dozen feelings, but she couldn't explain them to you if her life depended on it.

2. How it got there: Hey, she can't help it. Do you think women *like* having to go through this? "Just once," said my (Mike's) wife, Nicole, "just once I wish you could experience my period."

3. What to do—husband: Until menopause or a hysterectomy, you need to know *exactly* when "those days" are. Be extra nice and understanding, and remember to pray for your wife.

What to do—wife: Track your period as well so you can give your husband early warning; otherwise he'll probably forget. Also, don't let your menstrual cycle be an excuse for treating your husband like dirt. If you seek his forgiveness, he'll probably be so surprised that he'll do anything for you.

WHAT MORE CAN A HUSBAND DO?

1. *Esteem her character.* Gerry Parker says, "My wife's compassion and buoyant spirit is much more important than her hairdo. I'll take pains to comment about her good works. She appreciates that I've noticed."

2. *Never say, "Go ahead and have one more brownie, it looks good on you."* Those are fighting words. For many women, physical appearance is all-important. Instead, *look* for ways to compliment her. Perhaps you can even put them in writing!

3. *Encourage the best in her.* One woman told us, "I tend to be somewhat insecure in my abilities to accomplish things. My husband always encourages me to reach out and take a leadership role. He sees something in me."

   Men, we have a tendency to think the world revolves around *our* accomplishments—and that the wife will feel good about herself if *we* succeed. That's far too limiting. Instead, encourage her in areas that *she* can succeed in, such as a home-based business, serving in the church, developing friendships, and going back to work.

4. *Be a "construction engineer" with your words.* One man told us a story about the power of a well-placed destructive word. "A short time ago, I watched the venerable Sands Hotel in Las Vegas reduced to rubble in twenty seconds, all accomplished with a few critically

placed sticks of dynamite. Knowingly or unknowingly, we can do the same thing in our marital relationship. With a few critically placed 'verbal blasts,' we can tear down our wives' self-image—and our marriage—in a matter of minutes, although it took years to build."

This is especially true if destructive words are spoken in front of other people. Never tear down your mate in front of other people—NEVER!

5. *Don't build her up to get something.* Several men admitted they always said nice things to their wives for one reason: to get sex. If she is happy and feels good about herself, they reasoned, then they would get what *they* want. Bad form, guys. We'll boil down our advice to one sentence: A man should build up his wife because she deserves it, not to get something in return.

6. *Think of ways to protect her.* Steve Haskett's mother-in-law was a power-hungry person who never stopped trying to manipulate her daughter's feelings. "When I find out Shelley is going to spend time with her," said Steve, "we talk through what's going to happen. I'll remind her that when her mother says something negative about her appearance, she's to ignore it and change the subject. Shelley tries, but her mother is so persistent that she can still reduce her to tears by the end of the day."

7. *Affirm your wife's role with you and the children.* Rich Flansburg's wife isn't sure whether she's a good mom for the kids. "I hear that a lot from her," said Rich. "She asks me, 'Am I giving them all they need? And what about you? Do you feel loved and appreciated by me?'

"I always reply, 'You're awesome! You walk on water!' And I mean it. I wish the kids would appreciate how much she does for them. It's never hard to affirm her if she's genuinely trying, and that happens 95 percent of the time!"

8. *Talk to her.* Especially when the kids are in the infant and preschool stage, she needs adult interaction. She

wants to hear about your day. Not just the recitation of things that happened, but *how you felt* about the sales presentation or the rude customer.

9. *Finally, remember that her number one need is security.*

Women *hate* to drift in a sea of uncertainty. "For me, security means I know my husband is faithful," said Sue Wong. "I don't have to worry about worldly temptations for him. I can't imagine living a life wondering what my husband is up to if he is twenty minutes late."

When Jean Brinkley married in her midtwenties, she felt secure for the first time since she had left home. "When you are single, there's a big bad world out there," she said. "I had a car I was trying to pay off, a home I was trying to purchase, and insurance to worry about. I was always turning to my parents for help or asking some man to look at my car.

"There is a security in being protected as a female. You don't come home to a big empty house, and there is someone who is going to watch out for you, who will take you to the doctor when you are sick. After marrying Don, I felt protected, and that was a very good feeling to have."

Now that we've established this point, let us recap how a husband can build up his wife's security:

- Don't cut her down in public.

- Call when you're going to be more than fifteen minutes late from work.

- Avoid any disparaging remarks about her weight.

- Tell her she looks pretty after she's made an effort to look nice.

- Tell everybody that she cooks great and is doing a wonderful job of raising the kids.

- Give her an American Express gold card. (Wait a minute. How did this one get in there?)

WHAT MORE CAN A WIFE DO?

1. *Don't join in.* Amber Montrose has noticed that part of her husband's humor is based on self-depreciating remarks to make others feel comfortable. The trouble is, she would jump in with the crowd and needle her hubby in front of company. "At about our fifteen-year point, he patiently pointed out that he'd rather have my support than my retorts."

2. *Affirm his work.* Most men are motivated providers. Since few families are financially secure these days, many men worry a great deal. One husband said it well: "I struggle with the insecurity of our finances. I know God supplies, but it weighs heavily on my shoulders. The pressure is intense because my family is depending on me."

   Talk with your husband about your financial ups and downs, even if he protests that he wants to "protect" you from the financial strain. Suggest steps you can take to spend less. He'll appreciate your efforts.

3. *Shore up his weak area.* Marlin Roberts has an overactive thought life when it comes to sex. He's admitted as much to his wife, but she ignores that weakness. In fact, their periods of inactivity sometimes shift Marlin's thought life into overdrive.

   If a husband is honest enough to *share* this struggle, he needs your understanding. Men feel like men when their sex life is consistent. In your weak areas you want forbearance and understanding, right? He needs the same. And it's not just intercourse he's after. We all need daily hugs and kisses to remind us that this is a marriage, not a platonic relationship.

4. *Thank him when he does the expected.* Whether it's yard work, chores around the home, or working forty to sixty hours a week, men respond to genuine appreciation. They struggle as much as women, wondering if their lives have significance.

A "DARK AGE" HUSBAND'S TOP TEN ALTERNATIVES TO SPENDING QUALITY TIME WITH THE WIFE

10. Going in for a prostate cancer checkup

9. Working in the yard

8. Calling Ma

7. Driving the kids somewhere—anywhere!

6. Getting a head start on the tax returns

5. Chris "Back-Back-Back" Berman and ESPN SportsCenter

4. Checking the crawl space for termites

3. Flea dipping the cat

2. Tightening bolts on the Taurus's muffler bearings

1. Installing a new gun rack in the pickup

Respect Doesn't Come Cheap

*h*owever, each one of you also must love his wife as he loves himself, and the wife must respect her husband" (Eph. 5:33).

There it is in black and white, wives. The Bible says you *must* respect your husband. In case you're not familiar with the meaning of the *R* word, here's a quick definition: "to feel or show honor or esteem for; hold in high regard; avoid intruding upon or interfering with." To sum up, God says you don't have to *love* your husband (although your spouse is directed to love *you*); you just have to respect him.

When it came to respecting husbands, our research arrived at a dramatic conclusion: 100 percent of the wives agreed with this biblical principle and eagerly put it into practice. Why? Because their attitudes were like this bumper sticker: God said it; I believe it; that settles it.

Well, not exactly.

That's because, guys, many of us have blown it when it

comes to earning respect. It's one of those attributes that quickly vanishes if we mess up and—depending on the "crime"—takes a *long* time to gain back. Just ask Dan Bennett.

About three years into their marriage, Dan and his wife, Samantha, dropped by their neighborhood video store in search of a Friday night flick. As the couple paid for their rental, the teenage girl behind the counter thought it would be entertaining to remind Dan of some of the past movies he'd rented. After rattling off the titles of several well-known Hollywood releases, she blithely continued.

"Let's see here," she said. "We have *Debbie Does Dallas, Part IV, The Thousand Lovers of Emmanuel . . .*"

Whoops. The young clerk realized she was reading off the raunchy titles of XXX-rated videos—and three people turned four shades of red. Samantha was embarrassed, the checkout girl was embarrassed, and Dan was REALLY embarrassed. Samantha smiled and assumed it was a mistake, but once they got in the car, she found out differently.

"What happened back in the store was true," said Dan, as he swung the car into traffic. "That stuff has a hold on me."

Dan poured out what had been bottled up inside for months: He craved hard-core porn. He knew it was wrong, but he liked the excitement of looking at naked women. Samantha felt used . . . cheap . . . and wondered how many times Dan fantasized that "Debbie" was with him as they made love.

"I was really hurt that night," said Samantha. "It told me I wasn't good enough for him." She had every reason to be hacked off and view her husband as a contemptible creature not worthy of her respect. If a husband is using pornography, it's probably an addiction. And it happens with more Christian men than you would imagine (we read our mail at Focus on the Family). When the wife finds out—and she *will*—the fallout can devastate a marriage.

Dan never felt lower in his life. "It was like I committed adultery," he said. "After I confessed everything, I'm certain I lost her respect. At that moment I decided to be up-front with her about everything. I also began meeting with a group of guys who would help keep me accountable."

The proactive measures didn't go unnoticed by Samantha. After a period of time, she could see that Dan was truly contrite, and she forgave him. "I don't dwell on it anymore," she said. "The hurt is gone."

Moving On

Eight years have passed since that regrettable night in the video store. What lessons did Dan learn?

"You can regain lost respect if you're honest about every-thing . . . regardless of the immediate pain," he replied. "You also find out how strong your marriage is. If the marriage is strong, then honesty—even amidst a sin that could divide you—will make it stronger. Of course, you have to walk away from that sinful behavior, or that will worsen matters."

Vicki Closs says their marriage faced a stiffer test than "dabbling in pornography" sin: another woman.

"Out of the blue, Rob told me a gal at work was after him—and that his mind had toyed with the idea of an affair. He's the type of man where a lot of women are drawn to his personality and charm.

"Immediately, my respect for him went way down. I was

r several days. I felt very insecure. But Rob wasn't
, and he didn't try to weasel out of taking respon-
r allowing his mind to play around with the idea.
Fortunately, he hadn't acted on the temptation. I suddenly
realized I wasn't the only woman in the world. Because he
came to me and laid out the entire situation, I felt he valued
me and the marriage."

Rob continued to keep the communication lines open.
He gave Vicki the freedom to ask questions anytime she
wanted. He shared what goes through a man's mind regard-
ing lust and pornography—how he was wired. The revela-
tions surprised Vicki. "I think I was like most women:
totally naive. Not anymore."

What made the whole situation work was Rob's excellent
attitude. He was humble and matter-of-fact—"Here's what
happened, honey." That kept his wife in his corner. Rob
could have rubbed the news in her face: "Guess what,
sweetheart? The new account executive at work has the hots
for me. I guess it's just a cross I'll have to bear. In the
meantime, I'm going to remain faithful to you. That seems
like the right thing to do."

Such a pitiful speech would have chopped Vicki's self-esteem
off at the knees. He might as well have said, "I'm God's gift to
women. It's amazing I haven't had twenty affairs by now."

Instead, Rob took the high road. His honesty won him
respect.

Honest Deceit

As relationships move into the second decade, men often
become more "sophisticated" about hiding sin. They've had

a few years to study their wives, and not wanting to lose respect, they learn the art of hiding things. Not even clergy-men are immune.

"As a pastor, one of my top priorities is to be an honest man," says Kent Rogers. "I've asked God to make me ultrasensitive to occasions when I might lie—and he has! Because I've made honesty such a high priority with the Lord, I've naturally been tested and tempted. My chronic problem has been manipulating the truth. It's not that I tell total falsehoods; it's just that I leave out or add something that creates the wrong impression."

The line of truth can sure wiggle when we want it to.

On many occasions, especially on Saturday nights, Kent has asked his wife's forgiveness for past indiscretions: "I can't preach without having things right between the two of us."

And how does Dawn feel when she discovers her well-respected pastor-husband hasn't been on the up-and-up with her?

"I have lost respect for him when I've caught him," she says. "It's not the pattern of his life, so that helps. Seeing him repent and be sorrowful makes it easy to respect him again. I realize that the more successful he is in the church, the more the enemy wants to destroy him. So we talk about those things that might bring him down. We know that the seeds of big sins begin first as little sins that go unreported and unrepented."

That statement is not only true for pastors, it's true in all marriages. It's easy to forget that the enemy wants to destroy *your* marriage. If he can do that, then the chance of *your* children rejecting their faith and having dysfunctional families of their own is much greater. But couples who stick it out through the Dark Ages can pass along a legacy of faith, which has ramifications for generations.

Time-out for a quick question-and-answer session.

Q. *When are the seeds of destruction planted?*

A. *When sin is hidden, large or small.*

Q. *What happens if a husband doesn't have his wife's respect?*

A. *The father's role isn't lifted up in front of the children. She learns to rely on herself. The marriage is strained, and everyone loses.*

Q. *What should men do to maintain the respect of their wives?*

A. *Since it is inevitable that a husband will sin, perform dumb stunts, and forget anniversaries during the course of the marriage, the best plan is to come clean—before she finds out. If Dan Bennett had told his wife about the X-rated movies before she found out, there still would have been pain, but the wounds would have healed faster.*

Bill Sheedy, an Ohio pastor, has sat across the counseling table from hundreds of married couples over the past twenty years. He says the way a spouse finds out about sin is a harbinger for the future of the marriage. Were they caught, or did they confess?

"The marriage has a better chance of healing if they confess, no matter how many years after the fact. Whether it's affairs, prostitutes, pornography, lying, or spending money, it's better not to hide it. If the wife finds out on her own, the dynamics of the marriage are changed. They'll both know he betrayed her, and that *will* hinder their ability to be intimate."

Kent Rogers, the pastor who fiddled with the truth,

concurs. "Even though I'm embarrassed—'*I can't believe I did it again*'—my wife likes it when I cough up. My fear, of course, is that if I come to her with my latest transgression, I'll lose face. It never ceases to amaze me that just the opposite occurs.

"Besides, if a guy waits until he gets caught, there's a greater chance that the confession will be bogus. That is, he may *seem* to be broken and repentant, but he's aware of what his wife *wants* to hear—so he says it. Later, he'll act resentful when she asks questions about where he was or what he was doing. He shifts the blame to his spouse, as if it's *her* problem. The woman's dilemma is that she stops trusting him because he hasn't built up a bank account of trustworthy behavior.

"The best solution occurs when the husband takes responsibility for his wife's inability to trust him. If she flashes back and acts suspicious—maybe even unnecessarily—he's got to swallow it and realize he created the mess in the first place. He will have to own his mistakes. The men who do that will see their wives—and marriages—heal."

Cleaning Things Out

If a man loses the respect of his wife, it often occurs between the five- and fifteen-year point of their marriage. How does it happen? In two ways:

• *As we've already illustrated, he got caught with his hand in the cookie jar.* Because he didn't confess on his own volition, she may accurately conclude more is hidden. That'll shake her trust in him—and her respect. If the husband doesn't come clean, the marriage will stay in the Dark Ages.

- *The husband becomes a "professional procrastinator" when it comes to his own spiritual health or that of his family.* This is tougher to spot, but it is actually more common.

Though no one knows it but him and God, the hidden root of this spiritual neglect is mistakes that haven't been exposed to the light of God's truth. Hidden sin always creates problems.

While the husband's passivity toward pursuing spiritual things increases, his wife becomes chronically discontented in the marriage, often by the lack of direction shown by her mate. As her respect ebbs, they begin to fight. In their frustration they lash out at each other. The wife may even tell a friend, "My husband is a spiritual blob. The problem is he agrees that he should be the spiritual leader, but he never does anything about it."

Discontent leads to frustration . . . which leads to disrespectful acts and words. . . . This is the sequence that slowly kills marriages.

Goals to Reach For

But what if a husband *wants* to come clean? How can he increase his chances for success?

We heard about an Indiana church that schedules a men's retreat every fall. Over several years, the seminar leaders have challenged the husbands to bring their secret sins to light—within the safe context of small groups where men feel secure enough to share things about their lives that nobody else knows. One year, seven men confessed to committing adultery. Some of these guys, who had been carrying that secret around for years, said it had been eating away at their guts.

Their spiritual lives were stagnant, their marriages in jeopardy, and their children were rebellious.

After the men got it out into the open, the conference leaders were smart: They had a follow-up plan. When the husband was ready to tell his wife about his adulterous affair, they arranged for close friends to take their children for a weekend. After the husband broke the news, the pastors suggested to the wife that she refrain from telephoning her mother, sister, or best friend for "support" (which often fueled the fires of indignation and resentment). Instead, the pastoral team offered to counsel her or be available as she went away by *herself* to seek the Lord.

In all seven cases, this strategy helped the hurting wife to hear from God first. Coupled with counseling afterward, every marriage was restored!

Not every man at the retreat, however, felt comfortable lifting the hood and letting the world peer in. In fact, several men left that church because they felt resurrecting old sins wasn't necessary. Since God had forgiven them, why bring it up all over again and hurt their wives? They have a small point, but sadly a price has to be paid for this type of thinking: *If we walk in the light, as he is in the light, we have fellowship with one another, and the blood of Jesus, his Son, purifies us from all sin (1 John 1:7).*

These men won't attain a Renaissance with their wives until they bring their lives to the light.

The Big Fear

Will all wives respond with forgiveness and forgetfulness when they have that fateful conversation with their husbands? The answer is no, and it's that fear—a justifiable one—that keeps men living with their sin, women living with a lie, and the marriage light-years away from the Renaissance.

What can be done to alleviate this fear?

Wives need to find a place of security where they can be open about their own fears for "the worst," and yet still be committed to stay with their husbands no matter what. A wife can learn to respect her husband all over again, as it happened in the Henderson household.

"We had been married for about ten years, and I knew something was wrong," said Jill. "Mark is such a proud man, though, so it's tough for him to admit mistakes.

"One afternoon I was listening to a speaker at a women's retreat talk about giving your husband a Day of Jubilee; a day of forgiveness for all 'debts' our husbands may have built up in the past."

Stop the tape: *The Day of Jubilee is an Old Testament concept. Every forty-nine years, the Israelites forgave all debts, no matter how big or small.* Jill continued:

"She said not every woman could do it; it may mean some deep things come out that we would not be able to handle at this time. But if we could emotionally and spiritually deal with our husband's sins—even the worst possible scenario— our marriage would have a strong future."

That's if the man's repentance was genuine and he forsook his sin, of course. She continued:

"I sent the children off to spend the night with friends. When the time was right, I told him what the speaker had said and assured him I was in a position to deal with anything he had to reveal. He was kind of stunned. After thinking about it for a minute, he said he had nothing to confess.

"Six months later, still sensing things weren't right, I gave him the chance again. This time it came out. He told me on three business trips he'd visited a massage parlor. No actual intercourse had taken place, but he didn't try to soften the fact that he had gone too far. He called it adultery, even though perhaps technically it wasn't."

Jill admits it wasn't easy to handle that her husband had found sexual pleasure with another woman, but she was committed to him—and the marriage. They went into several months of counseling, which brought out other things that Jill didn't know about.

Mark said that once he began leveling with his wife, he wanted to come completely clean. "I loved her and our children too much to throw it away," he said. "My problem was I got into the wrong thought patterns. Once I got in deeper, I didn't know how to get out. If Jill hadn't given me the freedom to confess, I probably would still be trying to get away with things."

Again, we don't recommend the "jubilee" concept for every couple, but it is an idea to consider further or discuss with your pastor.

The First Steps
If your marriage is deep into the second decade, but you sense it slipping away, it's *imperative* you take action.

Men, ask yourself these questions:

• Is there any sin against my wife that has not been confessed?

- If I continue to live in this darkness, will my sin be uncovered? How will it affect my long-term relationship with my wife?

- Am I ready to forsake my sinful ways, or do I still want to continue this "season of pleasure"?

- When would be the best time to tell her?

- And after my disclosure, will my pastor and other men in the church support, encourage, and hold me accountable so I can have the strength to sin no more?

Women, ask yourself these questions:

- Am I committed to the marriage—and my husband—no matter what?

- Do I understand that if he has committed dark sins, it's not my fault?

- With help, am I willing to reconstruct this relationship to honor the Lord and regain respect for my husband?

- Does my husband need a Day of Jubilee?

In case you haven't noticed, this chapter has been totally one-sided. Though it's *not always* the husband who does something to lose his wife's respect, it usually is. Satan knows that if he can keep men bound up in darkness, he can not only prevent the marriage from reaching a Renaissance, but he may also be able to shut it down completely.

Respect is no small issue. Like reputations, it's hard to gain and easy to lose. If your relationship is lacking respect, ask yourself the above questions, pray about them, and then take the biggest step you're able to.

WHAT WIVES SAID ABOUT RESPECT

- "A husband who can provide a steady income is a big deal for women. We need to know we're being provided for. A couple who was in our wedding divorced because the husband was changing jobs every six months. They had three children, so when he was between jobs, she had to go back to work. I'm not saying what she did was right, but she couldn't trust him to put food on the table."

- "If he treats me and the children well when he's under pressure, my respect for him increases."

- "If serving God is a priority for him and if he's attempting to live the way that God says a man should live, my respect is always solidified."

- "He's encouraged me to be my own person, to take time to do things with my friends. I've done the same for him. It's like we're saying, 'Because I love you, I want to be able to share you with others. I want to see you grow and be refreshed without feeling as though you're tied down.'"

- "I started a home-based business making crafts. My husband was showing off our 'production line' one day to his parents. The way he talked about it, I could tell he was proud of me. Though he doesn't do much of the work, he demonstrated a knowledge about it I didn't know he had. That means he was paying attention when I told him how things were done."

- "My husband commands my respect in two ways: First, he maintains a high standard of integrity in his career.

Second, he takes authority with the children. Not only does he stick to the rules, he also sticks up for me."

- "I didn't grow up in a very strong Christian home. When my husband and I are having a disagreement, my tendency is to push a little far. Instead of responding in like manner, my husband will simply say, 'That's far enough.' He doesn't yell, he just has this you-know-this-isn't-the-way-God-wants-you-to-be kind of voice. If he wasn't a man who really tried to obey God, that type of attitude would probably set me off even more. But it works. I respect him because he's been patient while God continues to mold my character."

WHAT HUSBANDS SAID ABOUT RESPECT

- "My wife used to be the brunt of my public, sarcastic jokes. Finally, I wised up. We promised that we'd never be critical of each other in front of anyone else. Also, we committed to defending each other. No one could take potshots at us anymore."

- "Losing respect happens when one person crosses the line, whether it's integrity with taxes, being honest with relatives, or lying to the phone solicitor. Whenever you say one thing and do another, especially in the presence of your wife, it can cause her to inch down in her respect for you."

- "When I act selfishly, I know I lose my wife's respect. Then when I don't confess that selfishness, I lose double-respect points."

- "Respect and trust are earned, while love is something that should be given freely. Many guys I've known usually try to earn their wife's love and have respect and trust given to them."

- "Respect happens when you're a man who keeps his promises."

• "Treat the wife as an equal person who has intelligence, worth, and value. A woman can tell when her husband is being chauvinistic—body language is a dead give-away. He needs to treat her as a joint heir. God's given her gifts and abilities to complement his. One job of the husband is to develop them."

When Life Has Let You Down

We had one question we didn't want to ask: Has your marriage weathered any unexpected family tragedies? It was a tough topic to bring up because we realized we could be talking to young parents who are in the midst of a difficult family situation. We wondered if our inquiries would pull the scab off old wounds.

I (Greg) know healing takes time; our family has suffered its share of scrapes and bruises over the years. Eleven years ago our first son, Troy, was born with a birth defect. He went through three major surgeries before the age of four to fix it. Fortunately, he doesn't remember the hospitalizations. But Elaine and I sure do!

When we watched the orderlies wheel our son into the surgery bay, our knees buckled. Would he come out of general anesthesia? How bad would the pain be? What would it be like being cut open? Elaine and I spent a ton of time praying together, and with God guiding the surgeon's hand, our boy was made whole.

Another event that rocked me happened in the mideighties, when my father suffered a heart attack at the age of fifty-five. I flew to Reno to be at his side, but he had already slipped into a coma. He lived only another week, however, and when he was gone, I had never felt emptier in my life. Losing a parent isn't an unbearable pain, but even years later, I still tear up when something reminds me of him.

Finally, just a few years ago, my mother's lungs stopped working when her emphysema acted up. She went into full cardiac arrest, which caused oxygen deficiency to her brain. Though she survived, she ended up with a condition called dementia. These days, Mom's short-term memory is bad, she goes through bouts of paranoia, and she is generally hard to be around. Her husband (my stepfather) and my sister are bearing the caregiver load since I live fourteen hundred miles away.

In each case, these family tragedies have brought Elaine and me closer together, and that has been a good thing. To help support one another, we have prayed *for* and *with* each other. I shudder to think what we would have done without having an almighty God we could take our troubles to.

It's a sorry fact of life that tragedies, illnesses, and setbacks happen to the best of families. We live in an imperfect world, where husbands die and leave behind young families, where innocent children develop leukemia, and where loved ones grow old and die.

As we researched this book, we heard from couples who said their marriages pulled closer when "minor" tragedies befell them. Here are some examples:

- *Ten years into marriage, a Montana woman began grieving*

for the loss of two children she aborted during her teenage years. She wasn't a Christian back then, but that didn't excuse her deeds, she thought. She went through postabortion counseling, which culminated in a memorial service. The aborted children were given names, and prayers were offered. It was a traumatic time for the young wife, but her husband never left her side.

• *A New Jersey couple's oldest son was in a car accident that killed his fiancée a week before their wedding.* While recovering, he rededicated himself to Christ. The parents? They learned that caring for an injured son didn't mean they could neglect their younger child—or each other. "Fortunately, my husband and I were close friends," said the mother, "or this tragedy could have torn us apart."

• *Seventeen years into marriage, a Texas woman suffered a debilitating illness that put her out of commission for two years.* On a good day she could get dressed; on a bad one she couldn't get out of bed. The marriage was put on hold, and their sexual relations came to a grinding halt. Her husband, however, weathered the storm faithfully. Since he had pledged his love to her in sickness and in health, he saw her illness as a two-year blip over a lifetime of commitment. When she was finally cured, he knew their relationship would be stronger than ever.

Perhaps a similar calamity has struck you and your spouse. We know it happens more often than we'd like. Each year at *Focus on the Family* magazine, I (Mike) receive several hundred unsolicited articles from parents struggling with heartbreaking tragedies: a four-year-old son with a brain tumor; a young daughter molested by a baby-sitter; or the tragic story of a son who was run over by a car. Anytime I think my life is difficult, these poignant stories remind me that there are families who have it much tougher than I. These are brave, courageous people.

How *do* these couples face life's difficult situations? How *do* couples respond when life has let them down? Do marriages move to a deeper level, or does the fissure cause a marital split? (We couldn't find this information in *Vital Statistics,* but we've heard that the death of a child or the birth of a handicapped infant is the springboard to many marriages ending in divorce.)

Before we tell some stories that had the biggest impact on us, we'd like to share two trends we came across:

• *There's no right or wrong way to respond to a tragedy.* Because few of us get much practice, we can't expect each person to react the same way. Some people need their "space," while others have to cling to their spouse. Some clam up, while others "have to get it out." Just as we all look different, God gave us different defense mechanisms to cope with tragedy.

• *Tragedies test the mettle of a marriage like no other ordeal.* A couple with a hemophiliac son in the first decade of marriage, for instance, will face a deeper Dark Age. Of course, we can't go through life thinking, *Well, today my daughter could get run over walking to school,* but we can take some halfway measures so any unexpected events won't catch us *completely* off guard. For those marriages that have yet to be touched by family trials, let this chapter promote discussion about how you might respond if a tragedy does strike your family. Who would you call on for support? Who would watch the kids? Have you prepared a will? (Every couple should have one stating their wishes for who will raise the kids and how the estate will be managed in the event of their simultaneous death.)

Every Parent's Nightmare

Like most parents, Joe and Sue West's high hopes for a happy future were tied up in their three kids. When God gives you those little bundles of joy, it's natural to weave their lives into the fabric of yours. Like many parents, they would admit in an unguarded moment that there were times they loved their children more than their spouse—even, perhaps, more than God.

When the Wests had been married for eleven years, the unexpected struck. Their four-year-old daughter, Marie, came down with some flu-like symptoms. The family doctor routinely prescribed some antibiotics and sent her home. When the illness persisted, however, more tests were run. The medical establishment was baffled. Then the unthinkable happened: The young girl slipped into a coma and died just seven weeks after the onset of the illness.

"The best way to describe what I went through," says Joe, "was a debilitating emotional reaction. Guilt crept in because I thought I was responsible. When she died, a part of me died, too. I can honestly say I've never totally recovered."

Who can blame Joe for wanting to shoulder the blame? Before his daughter died, Joe was a happy person, someone content with his lot in life. Afterward, he fell into a deep depression, which turned to anger. He shook his fist at God: *How could you—the God I serve—do this to me? Why couldn't you have taken me instead? Marie had her whole life ahead of her.*

Meanwhile, Joe checked out emotionally from the marriage; Sue did her best to cope. "Like Joe, I was devastated," she says. "But at the same time, I felt God would do something with our daughter's death to turn it into something good. Before her illness, I was the idealistic type. Toward the end of Marie's life, I was truly glad she didn't have to live in her body anymore. She had lost all of her speech and movement. It was awful to see an active four-year-old lie motionless in a hospital bed. I didn't feel a whole lot of anger, just an emptiness."

Sue tried to carry on and be a good mother to the other children, but she couldn't bring herself to talk to Joe about the buried grief inside her. They shunned a counselor, too. Too painful, they agreed.

"At times I'd fight through my depression to draw Sue out," Joe says, "but all she'd do was cry. I decided the best choice would be to let it go and not talk about it, hoping that would make matters better."

"Joe's right," says Sue. "I did a lot of crying. But much of it was in response to his depression. I didn't know what to do for him, so I let him vent. I've always been an acceptor, he's always been a questioner. I didn't do any screaming, in keeping with my personality. But Joe dealt with it on a much deeper level; that's what he needed to do to survive."

Time is often the great healer when couples suffer the loss of a child—who expects to outlive their children? Though couples are quick to admit they're never the same, most learn to make baby steps to accommodate the pain and get on with their lives.

The Wests' attitude improved when Sue became pregnant and delivered a healthy boy, Robert. But a few years later, the unthinkable happened again. At about four years of age, Robert began developing the same flu-like symptoms that preceded Marie's death.

"I really wasn't prepared to lose another child, or even go through the threat of it," says Sue. "Though I thought I had 'dealt' with it the first time around, I hadn't had the knock-down, drag-out with God that Joe had."

The couple—along with a battery of doctors—fought hard against the physical changes that were transforming Robert from an animated preschooler to a weak, bedridden boy. He survived, but the ailment left him with a number of mental and physical disabilities.

For Sue, watching a second child suffer a life-threatening disease was too much to handle. "Emotionally, she was a shell," Joe says. "She had no feelings left, and things never really improved after Robert partially recovered. Though she did her best in the years afterward, she had no real interest in any form of intimacy, sex included. That part of her life no longer mattered to her, and who can blame her?"

It's been five years since Robert's illness. Sue's yet to make a 100 percent emotional return to her husband. Sure, some progress has been made, but her heart hardened from all the pain. It will take awhile for a complete thaw. In the meantime, they remain committed to each other, although the flame of love barely flickers. "Today, the greatest threat we are facing is cynicism," says Joe, "the feeling that nothing matters anymore."

What We Learned

If grief could be measured (and it can't), it's doubtful many of us will face one-tenth of the pain the Wests have gone through. But what lessons can they teach us about dealing with a crisis at any level?

• *Don't neglect each other.* As a coping mechanism, Sue and Joe immersed themselves in their marital roles—Sue with the kids, Joe with his work. They didn't make any extra time for each other—nor did they particularly care to. "We did grow a little bit together," she says, "but we didn't consciously decide that these situations were not going to be a wedge between us. Because of that, our daughter's death probably came between us more than we would like to admit."

• *Life is tough.* It sure is. You probably won't travel through life accident- or disease-free. While it's impossible to have all of your theological ducks lined up, your beliefs about God's favor and love for you shouldn't be determined by an absence of pain. (A book we highly recommend on this subject is Dr. Dobson's newest best-seller, *When God Doesn't Make Sense.*)

Sue went into marriage with her eyes open. "We both grew up in conservative Bible-believing families. I didn't think *everything* was going to be picture perfect, but I certainly didn't expect things to get this bad," she says. "I felt that if we were living a good life and trying to help others, we wouldn't get robbed of something that precious."

• *Try to uncover each other's feelings, no matter how painful.* Sue admits it was unhealthy for them to let each other try to handle the grief alone. Yes, you have to respect a spouse's desire for privacy, but you also have to talk. "We felt we didn't want to cause the other any more pain," Joe said. "We didn't purposely try *not* to share our feelings, that's just the way the course of our marriage went. Every wall in marriage is built one brick at a time. We didn't start out to build a wall; it just happened."

• *Your relationship will change—forever.* The temptation is to put the marriage on autopilot and to occasionally check the instruments to see where the relationship is headed. From the air everything may look fine—but the marriage has to come to earth some time. Reality will have to be dealt with, and that process shouldn't be put in a holding pattern for too long—or there will be a crash landing. Joe's love and commitment to Sue was strong, but when it was shaken, it was scarier for him to open up than it was for her. He made a candid statement to us, however. Joe admitted that the work it would take to achieve a Renaissance in marriage would take more than he's got to give—even ten years later. That's how difficult the process can be.

• *Your future doesn't have to be determined by your past.* The Wests told us they do expect their lives to be brighter in the years ahead. "We just haven't reached that crucial turning point," says Joe. "We're still raising kids and paying bills. There's very little joy in our marriage."

"Extreme tragedies," says Sue, "make for deep wedges. Our child's death did not bring us closer together. There is a tendency to fill the gap in your heart by looking outside your spouse and faith. I've found the tendency is to fill my life with other things: hobbies, shopping, keeping a home."

Joe does see the challenge ahead of him, which will be "to learn to love each other in a different, more mature way."

A Lump in the Throat

Married eight years and the father of three children, Randy Thomas thought life was swimming along nicely when he stood in front of the bathroom mirror shaving one morning.

He noticed a lump on his neck. *That's strange,* he thought. *That should have gone away by now.*

Randy, in his midthirties, walked into the bedroom. "Honey, what do you think of this?" he said to his wife, Kelsey, pointing to the growth.

"Hmm, I don't know, sweetie. Perhaps you should get it checked."

"Maybe you're right."

Things really started happening quickly after he arrived at the doctor's office. His physician thought he had a lymphoma—a form of malignant cancer.

"What are your plans for tomorrow?" the doctor asked.

"Go to work, just like every day," Randy replied.

"You better cancel those plans. We need to operate immediately."

The next morning surgeons performed a biopsy. Their hunch was right: Randy had Hodgkin's disease, a well-known, highly treatable cancer. Thus started a four-year road to recovery, which included twenty months of chemotherapy.

The family depended on Randy's paycheck, so he would get his chemo on Friday, be sick all weekend and Monday, and then return to work on Tuesday. He was credit manager for a landscape firm.

The idea of losing her husband caused Kelsey to think back to the day she stood before an assembly of family and friends and repeated a vow to love and cherish her husband "in sickness and in health."

"I was twenty-one when I made those vows, and I never thought I would have something like that happen so soon in our marriage," she said. "I thought illness happens when you're eighty. I wish somebody had prepared me to really consider those promises of loving a deathly ill spouse."

As Randy devoted his energies to getting well, the marriage went through a role reversal. Suddenly, Kelsey was responsible for maintaining the car, doing chores around the house, and working in the yard.

"I have pollen allergies, so when I pushed this big mower," she said, "it was a huge shock to my system. But Randy was too sick to help out. It was interesting for him to become the dependent person in the relationship."

When doctors informed Randy he was in remission, the couple noticed some changes in their relationship. "I feel much more able to get things done," said Kelsey, "and he is not so macho. Now that I look back, I can say the whole experience has been a positive one for us. I didn't mind looking after him. We also came closer together when we prayed for each other."

Unlike the Wests, the Thomases were able to avoid putting their relationship on hold. How did they do that?

"We realized we were going through something," responded Kelsey, "and we had to go through it together. I couldn't 'check out' until he was cured. We tried to continue our normal routine, like going on weekend camping trips, but that was very difficult because Randy was not feeling well. We felt strongly, however, that it was important to continue our normal family routine. Our marriage passed through a much quieter, tender time, and the relationship was strengthened."

Kelsey will never forget one event that spelled it all out for her. On one of their camping trips to a California state beach park, the two of them went for a stroll along the sandy shoreline. As they wrapped their arms around each other's waist and let their feet touch the surf, she saw a seashell in the wet sand. She reached down, picked it up, and held it against the setting sun. The alabaster shell was translucent, and the ocean water had smoothed the edges.

In the same way, Christ has smoothed the rough edges of our relationship, she thought. *I know the last couple of years have been tough, but this is a time to treasure what we have. Randy is terribly sick, and I don't know how much longer he will be here. I need to appreciate what I have.*

She pocketed the white, pearly shell and brought it home, where she put it in her daughter's collection jar. Every now and then, Kelsey looks at it as a reminder of that memorable afternoon.

What We Learned

It's hard to add to the eloquence of Kelsey's seashell story, except to remind readers that it took years for the ocean water to smooth over the rough edges. The same analogy holds when Christ is working in our lives, especially during a time of trial.

Parent Tragedies

Couples who are in the late stages of the second decade of love are often faced with choices of what to do with a parent who has a long-term or terminal illness. Since the adult child and his or her spouse rarely feel the same intense emotions, this can be a big hurdle for a couple.

When Teri Berg's mother discovered she had cancer, Teri reacted like most children would.

"I wanted to get on a plane and go be with her right then because my dad was in denial. My husband struggled with letting me go. 'What if it goes on for a long time?' he asked. It's not like he didn't think I should be there if she was dying, but in her case, she was months away from that. Eventually, he did say to me, 'I respect what you're feeling. Go ahead and go.'"

Knowing when and how much space to give a hurting spouse isn't always black and white. Hopefully, the situation won't go on and on, but with the Haleys from New York, it did.

"When Wayne's mother got ill," said Carmen Haley, "I thought it was going to go on forever. At one point she was living with us. Wayne even set up an intercom system. I remember she used to call him when we were in bed! For the next eight months, she went in and out of our home to nursing homes and hospitals.

"After eight months, I had had it. I finally told him it was her or me. She died a week later, before we decided to do anything. I just felt terrible. Wayne didn't hold it against me, but he could have."

Wayne picked up the story. "Carmen's right; it nearly destroyed our marriage. I felt I had to be with my mom a great deal. There's a special bond between mothers and sons, and I just had to do all I could. I probably put too high a priority on her, but it was a tough time for me. Afterward, it took awhile for the relationship between me and Carmen to normalize.

"I mourned my mother's death for about a year. That actually turned out to be a good thing. Carmen realized I had a sensitive side. The compassion I showed for my mother was the same I'll have for her if something ever goes wrong. She also saw me cry a lot. It broke down emotional barriers and made me a 'softer' husband."

What We Learned
Though it's impossible to predict every potential tragedy that may befall extended family, playing "What if . . ." isn't a bad idea. Before you get to the stage where older parents become ill, discuss how you'll react if certain things occur. Are there any circumstances under which you'd be willing and able to take in a feeble or terminally ill parent? What will you do if you have to make the choice between a nursing facility or in-home care? Planning ahead will help you avoid making snap decisions based on your emotions.

The Last Words
Tragedies have the potential to sap the strength and vitality from any marriage. Depending on the event, the Dark Ages can loom over a marriage like the shadows of a solar eclipse. If nothing else, we hope the illustrations in this chapter serve as a warning shot. We discovered that the best defense against the unexpected is a marriage where both partners are actively pursuing a growing relationship with Jesus Christ. Without that strong foundation, what you've built in the marriage could collapse if a load of pain comes your way.

Is There a Spiritual Leader in the House?

*i*t's Sunday night, and Rob Peterson is feeling the pressure. Ever since his church canceled services on Sunday evening, he feels responsible to lead the family in worship, devotions—something!

His supportive wife, Susan, is proud Rob is taking the initiative. Last week she overheard him asking a few buddies for ideas. For his first Sunday evening, however, Rob doesn't set his sights very high. He figures getting his three kids to sit still would be a major victory.

Rob opens in prayer, then asks, "What's the best thing that happened to you this week?"

"I didn't get a D on my math test," his oldest daughter replies sarcastically.

"I found a quarter walking home from school," pipes in his first grader.

"Some big kid on the playground tried to take cuts in tetherball," says his fifth-grade son, "so I pushed him to the

ground. He walked away like a hurt puppy. All of my friends gave me high fives for setting him down."

"Great," Rob says, shooting a glance at Susan.

"Don't look at me," she says. "I didn't get a call from school telling me he was fighting."

Rob collected his thoughts. After a brief silence, he says, "What I meant was, did God answer any prayers or do something that was miraculous for you?"

Silence.

"God didn't do anything for you all week?"

"Doesn't sound like it, Dad. What did he do for you?" his daughter asks.

"Well, um, I had to get this big project done at work. I asked God to help me finish it. I was about an hour away from my deadline—and a tongue-lashing from my boss— when I had a sudden burst of creativity. I finished it in fifteen minutes."

"How did God do that, Dad?" asks the youngest.

"Well, you know how God does it. He just does it."

"Oh."

A longer silence.

"Ah, well, Susan, will you read Psalm 23? Then I'll close us in prayer."

Thus endeth another episode in the continuing saga of *The Guiding Light*.

What do you think? Was Rob successful? After all, a godly father is supposed to combine the leadership of Moses and the preaching of Paul while the family hangs on every word, right? But what if Rob was a spiritual couch potato and his family *never* had any spiritual time together? What should Susan do?

- Remain quiet and hope for the best.

- Get on Rob's case until he's shamed into leading family devotions once a week.

- "Just pray" that her husband sees the light.

- Ask her pastor to coach Rob on what to do.

- Pick up the slack and lead the way so the kids won't suffer spiritual malnutrition.

Many of the wives we interviewed told us they had tried some or all of those five choices. Sometimes they worked, but often they didn't. These wives were hamstrung by the conservative Christian notion that the man, the biblical head of the household, leads by doing something "spiritual."

But what is "spiritual leadership"?

Is it Dad always praying at meals?

Is it Dad regularly gathering the family together for devotions? (By *devotions,* we mean a formal time of reading and discussing the Bible or spiritual-type books.)

Is it Dad reminding everyone that tomorrow is Sunday, time for church?

Is it *being* a good example? Or is it *doing* spiritual things? And if it's the latter, what are they?

Final question: Is it *really* the man's job?

I (Greg) asked myself that question, too. Elaine and I dated for nine months before I became a Christian in my freshman year of college; she was already a believer. When we were reunited the following summer, Elaine sat me down and said if we were going to marry one day, then she wanted me to be the spiritual leader of the home.

"Huh? What's that?"

Well, Elaine wasn't certain herself, but she thought it had something to do with me initiating Bible reading.

"How do I do that?" I asked. "What do I read? Do I have to talk about what I just read? How long should it go?"

We were game, though. We stumbled through Ephesians for several weeks, but our devotional time tailed off, as it has for the last twenty years. Sure, we've worked our way through several books for couples, but we don't read the Bible *together*. So you tell me: Am I a failure at being a "spiritual leader"?

I don't think so. Elaine knows how committed I am to Christ, and I know she's up every morning before dawn spending time with the Lord. The jury is still out on how our kids will turn out, but they know we place a high priority on prayer and the Bible by our example.

TOP TEN WORST EXCUSES FOR NOT ASSUMING SPIRITUAL LEADERSHIP

10. "If I tried to be the spiritual leader, my wife would say, 'What do you know?'"

9. "I flunked Sunday school."

8. "The wife insists on using the New American Standard, but I prefer the NIV."

7. "Our pastor says it so well."

6. "My dog ate my Bible."

5. "My most inspirational illustrations come from *Star Trek: The Next Generation.*"

4. "Dr. Dobson has already covered everything I wanted to say."

3. "Didn't Proverbs 31 say something about men 'sitting at the gate'?"

2. "With sixty-six books in the Bible, where do you start?"

1. You might be so good at it, she'll suggest you become a pastor. Taking a pay cut wouldn't be good stewardship.

Absolute Confusion

A New Year's resolution.

Another round of failure.

Guilt.

One man summed up the mantra we heard from many others: "I always had a this-isn't-the-way-it-oughta-be feeling. Though my wife and I get on our knees when there's a crisis, I have never initiated regular prayer. Hey, it's tough enough to get to church on time."

Our interviewees told us the topic of spiritual leadership created more confusion than nearly every other area of marriage. Their bewilderment fit a consistent pattern: prodding by the wife . . . several halfhearted attempts by the husband to do *something* . . . failure . . . more reminders from his wife . . . a few more attempts by the husband . . . more failure . . . resignation by the wife . . . relief by the husband . . . resentment by the wife . . . and guilt by the husband.

Many couples rationalize that it's best to forget about spiritual leadership and move on to other things. Sorry, we can't let you off the hook. While we have some answers, none of them are the black-and-white variety.

First off, men *are* given the biblical responsibility to be spiritual leaders, but their wives can play a big role to help them along.

Jim Harney, one of the several pastors we spoke with, said, "The Ephesians 5 model of Christ being head of the church and the man being the head of the home is the key. Admittedly, Jesus wasn't hamstrung by sin like we are. That's why it's so essential that men clean up their own acts first. We're not talking perfection here, just progress.

"If something spoils the harmony, peace, and joy homes should have, the man must know how to take the lead. If necessary, he needs to take the initiative to ask God's forgiveness, be it through fasting, prayer—whatever it takes to set things right. Why? That's the example that Jesus gave us. He did what it took to make us whole with God, and it cost him his life! It crucified him.

"All the Bible reading or family devotions is frosting on the cake compared to laying down your life. If a man will take that type of leadership, then praying and leading devotions will become spontaneous and automatic."

Jim's definition does two things: It takes the pressure off men and puts it back on them—all at the same time. It tells us we don't have to perform certain tasks in order to lead, but we do have to be willing to lay down our life for each family member.

"If a man isn't thinking of ways to serve his wife and family, he hasn't dug deep enough to understand true leadership. Most husbands today want to know what the minimum is.

They figure if they're doing *A, B,* and *C,* then they're probably doing better than others. I've seen dozens of men who lead family devotions but absolutely fail as spiritual leaders; they are also terrible husbands and fathers. Some of the worst damage occurs when fathers are doing the evangelical Christian leader thing and using it as a cover to stay in control, rather than serving their wives and children."

WHAT IS A "SERVANT-STYLE" LEADER?

Please excuse our use of jargon, but a "servant-style" leader is someone with a Christlike attitude who performs some of the following deeds:

+ Gets up before dawn and leaves for work so he can be home by five o'clock to spend time with the family

+ Helps with the dishes instead of reading the mail

+ Fixes a bike tire in a freezing garage after dinner

+ Plays checkers with his daughter when he'd rather watch *Monday Night Football*

+ Gets out of bed after the lights are out to reset the thermostat

+ Asks his wife if there are any chores she would like done, even though his own "To Do" sheet is as long as a grocery list

+ Helps with the kids' homework before his wife asks him to pitch in

+ Takes the initiative to follow through with the kids' discipline so his wife doesn't always have to wear the black hat

+ Thinks of new ways to put the family first

First *Be,* Then Do

Matt Norris, a veteran parachurch worker, says that "even when there's no guarantee of success, we need to step into the unknown and lead. For me, spiritual leadership isn't devotions, church, dinnertime prayer, or door-to-door witnessing. It's being transparent with my spiritual walk. My little boy studies everything I do. He even unbuckles his seat belt just before we pull into the driveway, just like me. Spiritual leadership means modeling the right actions and attitudes. Since my children are picking up nearly everything I do, I better be consistent."

One of Brent Hedley's house rules is this: *If you see Daddy doing something, then it's OK to do*; his two boys have heard him say that from an early age. For Brent, the idea clicked when he read Philippians 4:9, which says: "Whatever you have learned or received or heard from me, or seen in me— put it into practice. And the God of peace will be with you."

"What does that mean?" asked Brent. "It means in the way I talk to my wife, the way we decide arguments, the movies I see, the things I drink or don't drink—all these are things I try to live and set examples through, so there is no inconsistency with my family."

Lifting Up the Wife

Women who are cherished, built up, and protected by their husbands enjoy warm security. In fact, men who spiritually care for their wives usually aren't aware they are offering a form of long-term romantic love.

Just as sex is the guilt-producing part of marriage for many women, spiritual leadership is the counterpart for men. In fact, one woman told us, "My husband may feel closest to me when we are having sex, but I feel closest to him when we're praying together."

Many wives feel this way: *Having a husband take servant-style leadership seriously made them realize their husband could be trusted. And if he could be trusted spiritually, he could also be trusted with their deepest, intimate emotions.* And let's not forget the pure spiritual benefits of spiritual leadership. Dina Robinson hasn't.

"My husband, J. J., is studious in the Word," says Dina. "That's probably my weak point; I don't know the Scriptures well. Since reading the Bible is important to him, he has set a good example for me."

Laura Anderson is aware her husband gets up long before she does to spend time with God. "Andy's motivated to be all that God wants him to be. That spills over into the family, too. I've noticed when he has some bad attitudes toward me or the kids that he will feel convicted in a couple of days."

Andy understands that leadership is modeling the way. "I see it as pursuing a relationship with the Lord that is vibrant and exciting," he said. "If I'm not allowing Jesus Christ to lead me to become more like him, how can I lead my family? My wife can't make me arrive at a spiritual destination. I've got to want it for myself."

Juggling Multiple Roles

Christian men must spin many plates in the air as husbands and fathers. Yet some dads don't think through the consequences of how they spend their "free" time (the hours away from their job). Adding spiritual leader to the mix was just too much for some stressed-out dads, who placed more value on rest and relaxation. Don't get us wrong: We need some downtime, but leisure has to be in balance.

(Or does it? Actually, we think it's time for men to claim their right to veg out in front of the TV. There's enough pressure in most of our lives to fill an NBA play-off series, so women shouldn't expect us to be spiritual giants, *plus* be perfect at everything else we have to do! . . . Anyone detect some sarcasm on our part?)

Seriously, let's agree that we can't do it all. But let's also concur that if something needs to be cut to pursue servant-style spiritual leadership, it best be done.

"I see my role as leader, lover, protector, and provider," says John Bagley. "But my wife and two kids are natural leaders, so they buck me at every turn. At times I want to say, 'Go ahead and do what you want,' and then sit back and let anarchy prevail. It would be easy to do just that.

"But what I have chosen to do is make myself available to the family, which means I have to jettison some hobbies. That's been a real sacrifice. Talking to other men, I sense some resentment; they feel leadership isn't worth the price of forgoing a round of golf or a softball league. But there's no satisfaction comparable with being a servant-leader to your family."

HOW TO GET STARTED

Wondering how you can lead your family in a regular devotional time? Here are some guidelines:

- Try devotions after dinner at least once a week. Hungry kids and a frazzled mom trying to get dinner on the table won't be very attentive. Lead devotions after dinner but before dessert—the ice cream can be held out as a treat for listening!

• If your children are preschoolers or in early elementary school, read from a children's book that paraphrases the great stories of the Bible. Our favorites are two written by Kenneth N. Taylor: *Family-Time Bible in Pictures* and *Giant Steps for Little People* (Tyndale).

• Keep it short. Attention spans are short in young children. Five minutes for three-year-olds, fifteen minutes for elementary school kids, and a half hour for teens is probably the max.

• Use personal illustrations. Children *love* to hear parents tell stories on themselves.

• End with prayer. But ask for prayer requests first. You can also keep a little notebook and record how God answers them in the coming days. That exercise can make for a great spiritual lesson!

The Natural Way

Adam and Toria Brussels became Christians after several years of marriage—at a time when they were headed for divorce court. Not sure what to do next, they visited a Christian bookstore and purchased every resource they could find on marriage. They signed up for weekend conferences, listened to tapes, and watched videos—anything to get a better grasp on how to make Christ the head of their home.

What Adam learned, he knew in his gut: As man of the house, he *had* to look for ways to bring the lordship of Christ into the home. So how did he take that high concept and turn it into something practical?

Day in and day out in the Brussels' home, he and his wife began to talk about the Lord. They now discuss Scripture without setting a regular devotional time. Adam organizes Bible studies with other couples, and they open their home to overnight guests. "Our boys experience the Christian life just by watching us in action," he said.

Adam never *forces* things: Christian leadership is as natural to him as a long-distance runner reading up on the latest Nike trainers. Husbands who let spiritual discussions occur during the normal course of life often have secret admirers: their wives.

"Although my husband, Jerry, and I have rarely had a regular devotion time, he is a silent spiritual leader," said Kathy Jordan. "What I appreciate most is the way we openly share what we're learning about God. There is never any doubt that Christ is the center of the home. And Jerry's leadership isn't unnatural or artificial. He does an excellent job relating events from our life and circumstances to what he's found in Scripture."

Keith Fell says one way he leads spiritually occurs during his early morning walks with his wife, Marina. "We'll spend half the time praying as we walk," he said. "Our eyes are open, but we're still talking to God. We like to walk in the woods, where we're not inhibited by who might be listening. We will pray for certain individuals, hit various subjects, and then focus on home. It really goes back and forth, like tag-team prayer.

"Often, I'll find out something I didn't know, like a situation in Marina's life or with the kids in school. When we're done, I will ask her, 'Hey, why were you praying about such and such?' She will do the same thing."

Cami Carter, a pastor's wife, feels her husband's gentle approach is the best. "I'm a strong-willed, independent-thinking person. But the way he phrases things disarms me and helps me realize he's really wanting me to grow. He'll say something simple, like, 'Have you thought about this?' He works hard at not talking down to me. He also allows me to share ideas when it comes to spiritual matters. That lets me know that he's teachable, too."

But what if your husband refuses the reins of spiritual leadership? "Wives should ask him to lead, for starters," said Armistead Neely. "Nag, but in a positive way. Ask him, 'What are we going to do this morning?' Of course, you don't want to take cheap shots from across the room, like, 'This family is getting *no* spiritual leadership from you!'

"Instead, quietly challenge him to be a leader. When he does take a step, go alongside and support him. When he prays aloud at dinner, tell him how much you appreciate it."

If you happen to be in a situation where your husband is not a Christian, then you will have to take on the leadership role. That, dear women, can be the loneliest task in the world because of the lack of support—and possibly even ridicule. But if at all possible, you *have* to continue taking your children to church, teaching them what the Bible has to say, and involving them in church activities. If your husband comes around, fine, but if not, don't give up.

What Leadership Isn't

Listen, guys, we don't want to point fingers. But we do want to underline a few instances in which some men went too far with this spiritual leadership thing. Perhaps we can all learn from their mistakes.

"The perversion of spiritual leadership," says Chad Wall, "is to equate it with authority. When a man is big into authority, he's usually excused himself from taking responsibility for the family's spiritual health. For instance, some men like to think leadership is the authority to make decisions, instead of the responsibility to take care of his wife. Leadership is daily asking the question, 'What would be best for her?'

"First Peter 3 talks about a man granting his wife honor, respecting her strengths, and being humble enough to listen to her counsel. Leadership is never insecure. Nor is it always a privilege for the man, it's a liability. He's got the heavier weight."

Another wife wistfully admitted that she wished the family had had devotions together. "We've never had trouble praying together, but I think it's important for a husband to teach the family," said Susan Richey. "After years of feeling frustrated by a lack of spiritual direction, both Dave and I came to this conclusion: It's OK for me to remind him to do certain things that would open up discussion or allow the family to learn more about Christ."

Dave says, "It only took us about fifteen years to reach that conclusion! Why did we wait so long? Pride. Ignorance. Busyness. The feeling that *it was the man's responsibility to do something spiritual!* What a waste."

"Performance Christianity" Reinforced?

If one or both marriage partners believe it's the man's job to do the heavy spiritual lifting around the house, then they probably have a wrong attitude about their own relationship with God, as well. They're likely to believe that Christianity is *trying your best* to be holy and that the *only way* to do that is through daily prayer and Bible reading. *You get a star for every hour!* While these are certainly attributes of a godly person, they're only a means to the end, not the end itself.

Just as this regimented pattern of following God leads to a performance-oriented faith, so does the belief that "doing spiritual things" makes a man a spiritual leader. The weightier parts of living faith are "to act justly and to love mercy and to walk humbly with your God" (Mic. 6:8). The weightier parts of spiritual leadership are what we mentioned at the beginning: taking on the attitude of Jesus by your willingness to lay down your life and by making time to lead your wife and kids to higher ground.

And how can you tell you're on the right road? We think one dad found the key.

"We didn't have a predetermined family devotional time because I didn't like ours when I was growing up," said Damian Pretruccio. "But one time, when my son was in high school, he left a note on my Bible before leaving for class. When I asked him why he left it there, he told me, 'I knew you were sure to get it if I stuck it on your Bible.' I knew then I was being a good spiritual leader."

The Challenge
It was seven o'clock on the warmest evening of the summer in the Colorado Rockies. I (Mike) was sitting on the stage at the Promise Keepers event at Folsom Field on the University of Colorado campus in Boulder.

Everywhere I looked I saw men—fifty thousand of them. This was the largest gathering of males at one time, I heard someone say.

I could believe it. And with all that male testosterone out there, this was one raucous crowd. First, the men started a wave, and then one side of the stadium chanted: "WE LOVE JESUS, YES WE DO. WE LOVE JESUS, HOW 'BOUT YOU?"

The other side of the stadium wasn't going to sit on their hands. They returned the cheer but turned up the volume. Back and forth the chant went as the fifty thousand men screamed themselves hoarse. I wondered if the handful of gay-rights activists outside the stadium were going to drop their Hate Is Not a Family Value posters and make a run for it.

The final speakers of the two-day conference were Dr. James Dobson and University of Colorado football coach Bill McCartney. Dr. Dobson delivered a gripping address right out of the what-wives-wish-husbands-knew-about-women playbook.

McCartney, founder of Promise Keepers, challenged the men to be spiritual leaders, to "keep their promise" to their wives, children, church, and community. As a demonstration of that promise, McCartney asked all the pastors to come to the front of the stage. The stadium lights were turned off, and a hush came over the stadium. After a time of prayer, McCartney struck a match and lit a solitary candle. He held it aloft, and then reached down and lit a candle held by one of the pastors. He, in turn, lit the candle of a man standing next to him, and the scene was repeated over and over.

The small glow spread from the front of the stage and grew as it moved along the stadium floor and climbed into the stands. After twenty minutes, Folsom Field was lit by fifty thousand candles.

One of my friends told me afterward that the hair on the back of his neck stood on end. It was one of those spine-tingling moments that can change a man's life.

Can it change yours? Will you figuratively light a candle with us and keep your promise to be the spiritual leader of your home? If you can, you'll be joining a growing men's movement determined to be "promise keepers."

WHAT WIVES CAN DO TO HELP THEIR HUSBANDS LEAD

Whether a wife wants her husband to "do something spiritual" or "be someone the family can look up to," she plays a big role in encouraging her man to get off the dime. But how should she do it? That was a question we asked nearly every wife we interviewed. Here were some of the best ideas:

- "Women sometimes need to close their mouths, listen, and get to know the person God gave them."

- "Be on your knees for your husband. That speaks more than you can ever say with words."

- "Look for ways to build him up in what he *is* leading, whether at home or in his work."

- "Many men don't feel confident taking the initiative. Try to guide the kids to Dad when they're having problems. It can't be manipulative; it has to be genuine."

- "I know that my husband is a strong Christian, but he's

not verbal. So I'll start the conversation with the kids, hoping he will jump in."

- "One Sunday morning I was trying to get everyone to church. All Fred could do was lose himself in the sports pages. I told him in a calm voice, 'I'm fed up being the one to make things happen here. I don't want to be the only one getting the kids ready for church.' After that, Sunday mornings got better."

- "Being a spiritual leader is hard for men, especially if they're involved in church only on a surface level. I prayed for a long time that Ken would meet some other Christian men who could help him reach a deeper level. God answered those prayers, and he really started to grow in the Lord. When that happened, it was natural for it to flow out into the family."

- "John always leads the family in prayer. Then he leads just the two of us at night before we sleep and when we get up in the morning. And if he forgets, I remind him. 'Hey, are you going to say a prayer before you leave for work?' He doesn't take it personally or shrug it off. That shows a lot of maturity on his part. A wife can't expect her husband to remember everything all the time!"

- "Other ways to encourage him are by saying, 'Honey, I enjoyed it when we had devotions.' 'Sweetheart, would you lead us?' 'When you did that, it was great!' Those statements say that if he leads, we'll follow."

1 4

The High Calling—
and Cost—of Serving

g eorge, I want a divorce."

As those words shot across the restaurant table, George Myers stared at his wife in disbelief.

She's got to be joking, he thought. But the look on Donna's face told him, *This is for real, buddy.*

Few would have predicted George and Donna's marriage was headed for a cliff. The Myerses were an active couple who gladly served at their local church in a variety of ways. They were your basic pillars of the community.

Back in their early years of marriage, Donna was spiritually stronger than George. She knew her Bible, she freely volunteered her time, and she had great people skills. George knew he couldn't keep up, so he didn't even try. About fourteen years into the marriage, however, George caught fire. Years of plodding through Scripture paid off, and he actually began to enjoy memorizing passages and praying early each morning. When he joined a men's group, he was often asked to take the lead.

Brimming with confidence, George approached the church elders with an offer of help. He was duly appointed chairman of the Christian education committee, and he felt so comfortable that he was sure God was rewarding him for his faithfulness. Other people in the church noticed the new George, as well, and they slapped his shoulders with encouragement. The more strokes he got, the more he took on.

George took on a lot.

"Unfortunately," he said, "all this church work interfered with the home front. I ignored my wife and kids. At the same time she thought I was losing interest in her, another man in the church was paying attention to her—attention she wasn't getting from me."

With George gone several evenings a week serving at church, Donna was home alone playing the comparison game. When this man, a well-respected church leader, entered her life, she felt like a schoolgirl who had caught the eye of the class president. It wasn't long before "What if . . ." was swimming through her mind.

"When he called me the most wonderful person in the world," Donna remembered, "my heart melted. It's not that George was lacking, but I was caught up in this incredible excitement. I didn't really know what was happening at first. Since I had this fellow on such a high pedestal, I reasoned our relationship couldn't be wrong. Not only was he a charmer, but he was also a master manipulator who played with my mind. Every time I brought up some reason that our budding affair wasn't right, he convinced me God wanted his followers to be happy."

The romance progressed. They held hands, they embraced, they kissed, they did everything *but*. There was no intercourse; that was a line Donna said she never could have crossed. Still, Donna knew the relationship had gone too far.

"Obviously, my spiritual life wasn't much at that point," she said. "But in my mind I thought I could have it both ways: a relationship with God and a relationship with this other man."

The lovers' triangle caught the eye of the church pastor. One evening he called George over and broadly hinted that Donna was involved with another man. George rejected that notion out of hand. *My wife is a Christian. There's no way she'd ever do something like that.*

But there was a way, and the deceiver had lulled Donna into believing the answer was to divorce George and start over. Their three children? She and her new beau could deal with that.

Meanwhile, George ignored all the red flags. Marriage troubles didn't happen to "involved" Christians. But sitting in a restaurant and hearing those five words—"George, I want a divorce"—was like having cold water splashed in his face. Suddenly, George was in a battle for his marriage. No time for acting wishy-washy. As adrenaline kicked in, George displayed a steely resolve, a side of him Donna had rarely seen. For fifteen minutes the words poured out. "Tell me you don't love me!" he demanded. "I have to hear from you first. Tell me you don't love me."

Donna couldn't bring herself to repeat those few words. She *knew* she loved George; the other relationship was an out-of-hand infatuation.

But Donna had made plans to leave with her boyfriend

and the kids *that night*. The other man was even in the restaurant, watching from a nearby table!

She confessed the little scheme she and her boyfriend had plotted. George stood up and walked over to the other man. He told him in no uncertain words that he and Donna had pledged before God and man that they were going to be husband and wife for as long as they lived. "Your relationship with my wife is over," George announced forcefully. "I'd appreciate it if you never talked to her again."

The Myers gathered their belongings and went home. Within a few minutes, there was a knock at the door. The other man was standing there! He asked George if he could talk to Donna.

It took all his willpower not to slam the door in his face. Instead, George told him to leave and never come back.

"I made a spiritual stand that night," George said. "At that time, I was closer to God than at any other period in my life. I knew our relationship wasn't the greatest, but I had no idea this had been going on. God had been preparing me because I had stored a lot of Scripture in my heart. Plus, I was praying on a daily basis. Without that foundation, I might have lost Donna at the restaurant."

As they continued to talk into the night, George felt God was filling him with the Holy Spirit. "I did something I had never done before. I rebuked Satan and his demons, laid hands on my wife, and I prayed for her *and* our relationship. I knew I was fighting for my family's life; desperate times demanded desperate measures. I put off my hesitancies about spiritual warfare and just went for it." With a repentant attitude, Donna sought to restore her relationship with the Lord and with George. "I accepted God's forgiveness almost immediately, though it took much longer to forgive myself. I was pleasantly surprised how supportive people in our church were," she said.

What We Learned

Donna admits that George "always assured me of his love. He just didn't notice the warning signals."

Look for caution signals, folks. Days, weeks, and months can pass by in a blur. If your wife complains that you never take her out, she's not lamenting the lack of restaurant meals in her life. Actually, she's making a plea for attention. You would do well to take her out for a nice dinner—pronto.

When you're in the Dark Ages, the future can look cloudy. Amidst all of the distractions, it's easy for spouses to neglect giving time to the marital relationship. When that occurs, Satan tries to create some opportunities to fill the void. George got his strokes from heavy church involvement. Donna got hers when she was pursued by another man.

Feelings of neglect and fleeting thoughts of "there's something better waiting out there for me" have separated thousands of couples. Don't let the greener-grass syndrome happen to you.

The lesson here isn't to eschew serving. Rather, it's this: *The deceiver can use Christian service to cause one or both of the spouses to neglect each other. In fact, he can use anything. Be on guard.*

Calling All Friends

Jim Larner remembers the time an avalanche of church service buried him so deep he didn't even know he was smothered. How could he turn his back on Awana, the church board, or the growing youth department? He couldn't.

Frankly, his wife, Elena, was a church widow. His old friends never saw him. One night after dinner, they dropped by and did an "intervention" on Jim. Just like family members or a professional counselor who confronts an alcoholic with his problem, his wife and friends jolted him into realizing what he was doing.

"They said I was working and serving too much and not attending to the needs of my family," recalls Jim. "I felt shocked and betrayed—especially since my wife was the one who arranged it."

She was doing her husband a favor. Although the process was painful, it allowed Jim to poke his head above the clouds and see . . . they were right. He rotated himself off several committees, made himself unavailable for many meetings, and put his life back in balance.

Perhaps you've seen overcommitted church friends go through burnout—or terrible trials. Dozens of couples we talked with were involved in active service—whether with their church or local parachurch groups—but they struggled with the occasions when they volunteered once too many times. Since a spouse is purportedly doing "the Lord's work," what can a husband or wife say? That's why over-involvement in church work can be so insidious.

One survival key is giving your spouse permission to wave the flag when things are out of whack—and not dismiss his or her pleas for more time together. That's an arrangement the Matthews have made.

"Every six or eight weeks, we try to get away for an evening—a day, if we can manage it," Teresa says. "When Nathan's feeling the stress of a busy schedule, my life reflects it, too. That's one reason why I try not to get too busy myself. If I'm running as fast as he is, then I'm less able to notice when we're out of balance."

Like a battle commander who keeps some fresh troops in reserve, Teresa doesn't deploy all of her forces in the day-to-day stresses of normal family life. She holds something back; perhaps that's a smart idea you can use.

The Two Pyramids of Serving

Using the gifts God has given you—and seeing lives change for Christ—can be a heady experience. Sure, it's rewarding, but it can also be addicting.

Let's assume for a moment you're aware of some of the dangers, as well as these two things: (1) The second decade of love places great time demands on your marriage and your children; and (2) God has placed you in the body of Christ to be a blessing to others.

How can this be illustrated? Perhaps this drawing will help. Picture your marriage like two overlapping pyramids.

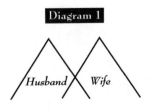

Diagram 1

Husband / Wife

The ideal is to serve in the church while staying in touch with your spouse.

As you can see, there's a slight overlap. This is the point where the husband and wife are doing things in tandem. It doesn't have to be a lot, just enough to keep them from living two separate lives under the same roof.

Elaine and I (Greg) have tried to keep this type of balance throughout our marriage. On a dozen occasions over the years, we have led a small group Bible study in our home. I enjoy using my Youth for Christ background to introduce "seekers" to Christ. I am also able to use my Bible college education to point out insights about Scripture. I love to lead an interesting discussion.

Elaine and I are a good team. God gave her the gift of hospitality, and she has put it to good use. She has always created a warm, comfortable atmosphere to make everyone feel at home.

For the last couple of years, however, we haven't led a Bible study. Why? Life has gotten too busy, and we realize that we need to save our free evenings to reconnect as a family—and as a couple.

Not that we've dropped our efforts to evangelize. What we've noticed is that our children's sports programs are putting us into contact with many nonchurchgoing families, and we've been able to reach out to our new friends. There's something about standing on the side-lines and cheering on our sons that makes for a great mixer.

These two pyramids also clearly illustrate how most of our time is spent apart. Elaine's managing the home, helping in the boys' classrooms two days a week (they attend a public school), and serving on the parent accountability committee.

My extra time (ha!) is spent writing in the early mornings and occasionally speaking on weekends. Life is hectic but not stressful. We manage to keep 80 percent of our evenings and weekends free for family activities. It's a balance we are comfortable with.

Gary and Marcia Bell have struck a balance in their home as well. "I used to think the way to serve God was by attending church meetings," said Gary. "I placed more value in that than I did in being a faithful servant at home. Eventually, we gave each other the freedom to serve where our hearts lead."

"Two years ago," Marcia said, "I ministered to a woman who was dying of breast cancer. I was home-schooling at the time, but Gary supported my desire to help this friend out. He knew how important it was for me to be available to her. He trusted me enough to go when I was needed— as long as I didn't consistently leave our family in the lurch."

Gary was her biggest booster. "Marriage is not only giving each other freedom," he said, "it's recognizing how your spouse serves best and encouraging her in her gifted areas. For instance, Marcia loves to wash someone else's dishes or clean their floors. She feels the Lord's pleasure in doing that. To demand that she just follow me and do what I want her to do isn't right. She recognizes that in me, too. I have the freedom to do what I feel is pleasing to the Lord."

Another View

Now, let's take a look at a second set of pyramids that illustrates two lives serving separately.

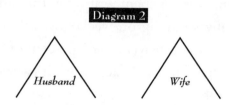

Diagram 2

Husband Wife

Though this arrangement is occasionally unavoidable, a prolonged period of serving outside the home will strain most marriages. If you find yourself falling into this pattern, ask some questions: Why am I serving so much? Is it because this is the only venue where I am appreciated? Has my spouse dropped hints that I may be doing too much? How have I responded to a plea for more time at home?

To prevent church involvement and service to others from keeping your marriage in the Dark Ages, you must develop a clear strategy. Here is a simple, yet effective start:

• *What are your spiritual gifts?* (Examples: leading, teaching, administrating, or giving.) What do you like to do? Write down areas where you are currently serving or would enjoy volunteering. Have your spouse do the same.

• *Is there some overlap?* Can you combine some areas and serve together? After you find areas of common interest, start serving together as soon as your schedule allows.

• *If not, what can be altered to change the present situation?*

Being in the Lord's service should be a win/win situation. Adults should want their marriage to be a model of servanthood. The reason? First, it's biblical. You're a member of the body of Christ, and therefore, you have responsibilities to serve. Second, your children—and others—need to see someone as an example of what true servanthood is.

In addition, you'll enjoy the fulfillment that comes from expressing the gifts God has given you. It's fun to be used to meet practical or spiritual needs. And finally, it can allow you and your spouse to spend more time together instead of apart.

See? It's a win/win situation.

Follow the Yellow Brick Road

g uys can be so insensitive. Ask a married man who his best friend is, and he'll probably mention an old college buddy, a longtime tennis partner, or a colleague from work.

Odds are he never thought of naming his wife.

That's too bad because she *can* be his best bud, whether he knows it or not. For some couples the second decade of marriage travels on a long, country road with a fork lying ahead. Those who've been "sticking it out" because of the kids have a clear understanding that some big decisions are going to be made when they reach that fork—usually a year or two after the kids have left the nest.

But those couples who have been tending to their *friend-ship* won't see a diverging path in future years. Instead, they'll see a single lane. Why? Because at some point earlier in the marriage they made a commitment to travel on the same road together—for better or worse. Their hope: that the third and fourth decades of marriage will lead them down the yellow brick road to marital togetherness!

So, how can your marriage get to Kansas?

By taking small steps down that road, of course.

I (Mike) recently saw a glimpse of what I want my future to be like with Nicole. On a business trip to Georgia, I spent some time with Richard and Dee Dee Stephens. I had met them a couple of years ago when I traveled to Columbus, Georgia, to write a story on a high school group called Teen Advisers for *Focus on the Family* magazine.

During a summer weekend with Richard and Dee Dee, I awoke to a quiet house. Walking out to the living room, I could hear the couple talking on a porch overlooking the Chattahoochee River reservoir, which separates Georgia and Alabama. I poked my head outside, and they warmly asked if I wanted to join them for a cup of coffee.

For the next ninety minutes we talked about their kids, my kids, my work, his work, and what we expected the future to be like. They told me how sixty Jet Skiers form a procession on the morning of the Fourth of July and parade by the river homes with American flags held aloft. The stories kept coming one after another. I was dumbstruck. Richard and Dee Dee *really* know how to *talk*. None of this superficial "good-buddy" stuff about the Georgia Bulldogs football team or the Tomahawk chop.

I asked Dee Dee *how* she and Richard became such good conversationalists. How had they developed their friendship? Was it hard to do? We've all seen older couples in restaurants eating their meals while barely exchanging a word. Though that could be the pattern they're comfortable with, it's likely that many old marrieds simply ran out of things to say when the last child left the house.

The short answer, Dee Dee began, is that she and Richard have been talking about *everything* in their lives for years. Like a regional reservoir that slowly fills with spring runoff in order to meet a city's long-term water needs, they started filling their conversation well seventeen years ago as they were coming out of the Dark Ages of their marriage. Today, firmly established in the Renaissance, they can tap into a lifetime of shared experiences.

"Our kids are leaving the nest," said Dee Dee. "The third one recently left for college, leaving just our fourteen-year-old daughter at home. We've had people say to us, 'Oh, won't that be awful when she leaves home?' But I'm not the least bit worried. There's a part of me that can't wait to be alone with Richard when she's gone."

During the Stephenses' Dark Ages (right around the eighth year) they were traveling in opposite directions. Richard was a car guy, a fellow who sold Fords for a living. Dee Dee didn't know the difference between a radiator and a distributor—and she wasn't interested in finding out. Although Richard loved his kids, he left the child-rearing duties to his young wife. While she kept busy with car pools and ladies Bible studies, he put in a long workday. The list goes on: He was a golfer; she was a tennis player. He liked to hunt and fish; Dee Dee's idea of the outdoors was sunning herself in a lounge chair while the kids played with the garden hose.

Nearing the end of their first decade, the pair attended a Marriage Encounter weekend, where they reaffirmed their desire to find some common interests, to *be friends*. This is what they settled on:

Each morning, after the kids had left for school, they would sit down and have a cup of coffee at 8:15. This would be the only private time of the day because their teens were apt to stay up later than they did.

They'd pour each other a cup of coffee and *talk*. No *Today* show interrupting their thoughts. (Lest you wonder if Richard is putting in a full day, he works from 9:00 A.M. to 6:00 P.M.)

The other "couple" thing they've learned to enjoy is *shopping*. Yes, the pastime that is the bane of every husband from Freeport, Maine, to San Diego, California, is something they love to do.

"When we travel, we like to check out the malls," said Dee Dee. "This is our free time, and what else are we going to find to do together? With a lot of couples we know, the men play golf while the women shop. We wanted more than that. The art of conversation didn't come naturally, though. It had been there when we were dating, but we lost the knack. We had to find it again, and then we had to work at it. Now it's not work anymore."

Did you catch Dee Dee's statement? Talking together "didn't come naturally." *It is something that needs to be worked at.* And that's the way we should approach our friendship with our spouses. We must cultivate it.

Where's Your Commitment?

Elaine and I (Greg) are committed to our *marriage*. We know firsthand the gnawing pain divorce causes. Both of my parents were married three times before I was out of

high school, and Elaine's parents split after twenty-five years. No matter what age you are when your parents divorce, it hurts.

Though we love each other and are committed to the marriage, have we been just as committed to building our *friendship* over our eighteen years? To be honest, no. It's only been recently that we've felt we had enough energy to invest in the friendship. It's a fact of life I deeply regret. It's not that we've been totally asleep under the same roof or living a relationship of convenience, we simply didn't intentionally pursue the friendship. After doing dozens of interviews with couples throughout the country, I learned we weren't alone.

Nearly every time I'd ask, "Would you say you're committed to the husband-and-wife relationship more than you are to the friendship?" I'd get silence. If I was talking to the eight- to fifteen-year married veterans, they'd finally say yes, they were more committed to the marriage than the friendship. If it was couples who had more years under their belts, most would say they were committed to both.

Here's the million-dollar question: *Can you say both?*

If you can, then you're likely experiencing a Renaissance. If you can't, then you probably aren't. It's as simple as that.

You've made it this far in the book, so we're going to assume you're tracking with the dilemmas we've mentioned in the previous chapters that keep marriage in the Dark Ages. We're also going to make a big assumption: You're ready for a Reformation and *really* ready for a true Renaissance. How is it achieved? Well, we could mention more communication tips and dating ideas, but until both partners *want* to pursue each other as close, perhaps even *best* friends, the joy in the relationship will fluctuate depending on when you spent your last night together without the kids.

Yes, getting away together—often—is part of the puzzle, but it's not the golden key: friendship is.

Remember our opening vignette in chapter 1? The one where the children had left the nest, and the husband and wife were finally alone? This is the point in life where the rubber meets the road. If the friendship hasn't been a major priority for several years leading up to that juncture, the next twenty to thirty years could be hell on earth. If you still have children coming and going through your front door on a daily basis, *it's not too late!* But it's time to get to work.

If you need a few ideas on how to do this friendship thing, we hope the list below will give you a head start. It did for us!

HUSBAND AND WIFE FRIENDSHIP IDEAS GUARANTEED TO GET YOU MOVING IN THE RIGHT DIRECTION

- Begin a habit of doing *something* together: researching your family tree, gardening, walking, browsing, driving, collecting, volunteering, traveling, cooking, or participating in sports activities.

- Cut back (not quit completely) on things that don't enhance your relationship: TV, hobbies, or sports that keep you separated.

- Join a club. Nicole and I (Mike) belong to the Swiss club, made up of families of Swiss immigrants. They have fondue nights, a Samichlaus get-together (the Swiss St. Nick), and an annual picnic.

- Make a point of talking every day, even if it's just for ten minutes. If your children are still small, you won't be able to "find" the time—you will have to carve it out. If it's a priority, you can do it.

- The *hardest* thing for couples to do is find time to talk. Lately, Nicole has been making iced coffee drinks at night. I'm not a coffee drinker, but this tastes like a coffee ice-cream shake without the artery-clogging calories.

- Eat lunch out. It's cheaper than dinner, and you can save on baby-sitting costs if the kids are in school.

- Several sports are good for couples: mountain biking (90 percent of bikes sold are the ones with the big knobby tires), playing tennis or golf, coed softball and volleyball, and bowling.

- Serve together through your church. This is another way to kill two birds with one stone by serving *and* spending time with your spouse.

- Each Sunday evening share your daily schedules for the coming week. Not only will you know what's going on, you'll feel more involved with each other.

- Meet other couples for Saturday morning breakfast or after-church brunch.

Finally, heed the advice a father gave one of his adult sons: "Treat your wife with as much courtesy as you would a friend, even a stranger. If you can treat her like a best friend, you'll be fine."

WHAT PEOPLE SAID ABOUT FRIENDSHIP IN MARRIAGE

- "Some couples are project oriented, and their kids are the current project they're working on together. When the kids are gone, many have nothing left. If the project of raising children gets in the way of the relationship, the project has become the priority, not the marriage."

♦ "For me, love is doing and giving to my wife what is best for her, even at my expense. Her definition of love is doing what's best for me at her expense. If only one person has that belief in marriage, that person's getting used. We've learned that the Scripture about laying down your life for a friend is a marriage verse."

♦ "If sex weren't involved, I don't know how interested my husband would be in working on our friendship, yet that is what I'd like to work on most." *[Ouch!]*

♦ "Friendship is the one aspect of the husband-and-wife relationship that makes the marriage work. It's not the other way around. Friendship is *the* component that makes the relationship strong."

♦ "My husband is relieved that I have girlfriends so he doesn't have to play that close friendship role. That's not good. I wish he'd crave more in our relationship. But I don't think he will. His idea of bonding is playing racquetball. When we're sixty-five, and all of our friends are dead or gone, we're going to be in big trouble. Today, our lives are full and I'm happy, but if we're ever thrust into a situation where we'll be alone, I know we'll be very unhappy."

♦ One of the easiest ways men avoid their wives is to play with their kids. What wife doesn't want that? It looks so noble. I think it takes more courage to tell your kids you're done playing and go to the kitchen and ask your wife how her day was. Especially if she gave you the international 'It's been a hard day, don't mess with me' look when you walked in the door."

♦ "Our friendship is something separate from what we do as parents. I don't necessarily believe that the only way to maintain a friendship with my husband is to take him away and have him all to myself. It happens in the midst of our home. I'm more up for that than most women I know. I gain much of my significance by my ability to keep our friendship strong in the midst of the chaos four children bring to a home."

- ♦ "The depth of our friendship comes in the absence of expectation. When I have close friends, there's nothing they have to do to perform to keep me as their friend. We've learned the secret of releasing each other from a rigid set of expectations."

16

Attitudes for Success

*i*f you're in the midst of the Dark Ages, we want to offer you some hope. *All* the veteran couples we interviewed—husbands and wives with fifteen, twenty years under their belts—said they were enjoying marriage as never before. From here on out, they chimed, it looked like smooth sailing ahead.

U.S. divorce statistics back them up, as only 8 percent split up after twenty-five years of marriage (see chapter 1). How did these couples get over that hump?

Attitude. Grace. Humor.

First off, many said they resolved early on that divorce was not an option. If the *D*-card was never in the deck, they pointed out, then it could never be played, even on days they didn't like each other very much.

Prior to their wedding, Robert Lilly can recall the occasion he and his wife, Patricia, decided up front never to get divorced. "We were window shopping one Saturday afternoon. I can remember crossing the street with Pat, and the issue of fidelity came up. We both agreed then and there we would always stay married. Nor would we go back to Mom or Dad when times get tough."

In a similar vein, Dee Dee Stephens heard this wedding-day advice from her mother: "If you get into an argument with Richard, don't call or come home. If you tell me about it, I'll automatically take Richard's side. You and Richard will have to work all your problems out." Although her mom may have sounded a little harsh on such a happy occasion, she was imparting excellent advice.

What We Learned

Make a special date with your spouse. Over a romantic dinner, ask him or her to make a vow with you that divorce will never be an option, even though there will be times when you can't *stand* each other. Perhaps the two of you can even bow your heads for a moment—yes, we know that's tough to do in public—and ask God to provide a hedge of protection around your marriage.

In Sync

Like a rookie-dominated NFL team that needs several seasons to gel, Leannee Flowers said it took a few years before she and her husband, Drew, became a team. "Now, after eleven years of marriage, I see us as two people united to be something that we could not be apart. I feel we have been through so much over the years—we're raising four children—that I don't want us to ever take each other for granted."

We could tell that Leanne felt *very* secure about her

marriage. "I never wonder if we'll still be together five years from now," she said. "My point is that I always want to be a wife that he wants to come home to. I don't want him to feel that it's a burden to be married to me."

No, we don't think you'll have that problem, Leanne.

Attitude can mean everything, agrees Deborah Camp. "Somewhere along the line, you, as an individual, are going to have to put everything you have into your marriage. When those hard times come, you know you've already told yourself you're going to stick with it."

Deborah said the start of marriage is like standing at the base of a mountain range with your spouse: It's hard to see what's beyond the summit. "At the bottom of the valley," said Deborah, "you might utter, 'I hate this situation.' In my case, it was the birth of our handicapped child, or the time my husband left the barn door open and all our chickens were killed. But somehow, we kept plodding ahead. Just making it through a tough family crisis gives us the confidence to continue," she said.

What We Learned

Just as an excellent attitude helps employees succeed in the workplace, so can a good attitude around the house make all the difference in a marriage. Are you a grump, or do you have a sunny personality? Are you a complainer or eternally optimistic? You'll never climb the mountain of marriage complaining every step of the way. It's too draining.

Take your attitude—or your spouse's—to the Lord in prayer. Just as he can change hearts, he can also change outlooks.

Saturday Night Live

Chris and Heather Alexander had a *terrible* first decade of marriage, but they never lost their sense of humor. When Chris was working three jobs—delivering 550 daily newspapers, waiting tables four nights a week, and doing janitorial work on weekends—the work load nearly buried him. So Heather, home with two toddlers, decided to cut the tension and play a practical joke on him.

One night, while Chris was working at an office, Heather bought her husband's favorite treat: chocolate Hostess cupcakes. She crawled on her hands and knees outside his office window and tied the cupcakes to the end of a long stick. Then she raised the pole and started waving it side to side.

When Chris noticed the dancing cupcakes, he burst out laughing. Said Heather, "That little stunt broke the tension. Believe it or not, that was a turning point in our marriage. From then on, whenever our communication got bad, one of us would do something really hilarious. Laughter is the one thing that keeps our marriage fun."

Heather got a joke returned to her shortly after the cupcake incident. One of Chris's friends had a stuffed armadillo (yes, the setting for this story is Texas), so Chris borrowed the critter and hid him in the hall closet. One morning Heather searched for some shoes and discovered this four-legged creature staring her down. She screamed and called her husband at work.

"Hello," said Chris.

Silence.

"Hello. Is anyone there?" he asked.

More silence.

Chris burst out laughing. He *knew* his practical joke had found the mark.

What We Learned

Look for ways to keep the marriage light. Adults laugh entirely too little. Sure, not every situation calls for a practical joke, but remember: "Laughter is medicine to the bones."

TOP TEN WORST WAYS A MAN CAN INSPIRE ROMANCE

10. Remember your anniversary—three days late!

9. Tell her she can pick out her own birthday gift—then hand her ten bucks.

8. Buy her a tear-away negligee.

7. Begin kissing her as soon as the lights go out.

6. Ask her to wear a wig during you know what.

5. Hum the tune, "I'm in the Mood for Love."

4. Arrange for the kids to sleep over with friends, then rent a "Rambo" movie.

3. Scream "yowsa!" as you browse through the *Victoria's Secret* catalog.

2. Go to bed naked.

1. Say offhandedly, "Halftime will work for me."

Watershed Years

Couples nearing the end of the second decade of love said any pretenses had been stripped away years ago. *What you see is what you get,* they agreed. Sure, a few burrs could be sanded down, but they realized they weren't going to be able to "change" their spouses.

Heather Alexander, of dancing cupcakes and stuffed armadillos fame, said after twenty years of marriage she *knows* she can't make her husband become someone he isn't. "There is nothing I can do," she said. "What I *can* do, however, is make myself a more pleasant person. I'll hear people say, 'My husband is acting like a jerk,' or 'My wife drives me crazy when she does this.' Chris and I don't have a lot of sympathy for that. What you need to do is ask *God* to change your mate and for you to be the person he wants you to be. I believe God honors that."

Heather, whose husband is now a church pastor, said they've both seen instances where a tired husband is insensitive to the needs of his wife, especially the mother of small children who needs a break.

"With marriage, you have to give and give and give," said Heather. "That's what it's all about."

When Karen Moore walked down the aisle, she carried different notions of what married life was going to be like. She had heard that modern marriage was a fifty-fifty proposition, and for the union to succeed, she and her new husband would each have to take half the load. Karen was also hoping that marriage would bring her inner stability. She was *sure* Marc would take her out every week because of his desire to meet her emotional needs.

Marc did his best. But weeks stretched into months at the Home of the Living Couch Potato, and the Moores rarely ventured outside. Being a homeboy was fine for him, but Karen felt life was passing her by. She yearned for adult conversation and an occasional escape from the kitchen. After months of inactivity, things got so bad that they agreed to see a counselor. Although Joe didn't cotton to "highfalutin' eggheads with Ph.D.s," several sessions helped the couple recognize one thing: Marc wasn't a plan-ahead type of guy. If Karen wanted to get out of the house, then she should make reservations instead of dinner.

The marriage improved dramatically after Karen stopped waiting for Marc to fill in the blanks on their social calendar. "But if I hadn't said anything," said Karen, "we never would have gone out or done anything together."

What We Learned

As a young bride, Karen held a worldview that marriage was a "he does his half and I do my half" arrangement. Fat chance. Jean Miller told us she went into marriage *knowing* it was a one hundred–one hundred proposition. "If I go the extra mile, I have a better chance that my husband will come back and do the same for me. If I go halfway, he will go halfway, and it ends up being a tug-of-war."

If you're putting only half your energy into your marriage—expecting your spouse to pick up the remaining slack—you're going to be one disappointed cookie. Did Michael Jordan leave half his talent on the court following a Chicago Bulls game? Could Chris Evert and Jimmy Connors perform at 50 percent and expect to win the U.S. Open mixed doubles championship? Of course not.

Stepping into Midlife

Dave Nelson believes the fourteenth year of marriage is

often a watershed anniversary. "Youthfulness is starting to disappear," said Dave, who's been married for two decades. "The time you and your spouse have been spending together has been adding up. The fantasy is over. You realize that who you are is what you are, and you are going to be with each other for the rest of your life. For some, a little bit of the dream has dried up."

In a sense Dave is describing the components of a midlife crisis. Those in the midst of their second decade of marriage are usually "celebrating" fortieth birthdays. Amidst all the black crepe paper and cutting humor, some forty-year-old husbands and wives are staring straight into the abyss. *Is this what I really want for my life? Is this as good as it gets?*

As I (Mike) write this book, I am a few months shy of my fortieth birthday. *Forty years!* Does that mean I should be gearing up for a midlife crisis?

When I put those thoughts to Dave Nelson, whom I've known for nearly fifteen years, I listened closely to his response. He said *every* time he drew close to the Lord, his life became exciting. If his relationship with God was moved to the back burner, he felt lost.

Dave, who is a pastor and a condominium manager, said he counseled many couples who became disillusioned after the kids arrived. "Unless they have something to focus them back in and are learning to see God in all things, they are going to grow apart." Dave said he and his wife, Stephanie, have brought Christ into the center of their relationship, and as a result, they are having more fun than ever before. "The barriers are down," explained Dave. "The areas of pride and ego aren't there. Sure, our bodies are a little older and the wrinkles are starting to show, but we're actually enjoying those wrinkles because they are marks of aging— marks we are sharing."

What We Learned
Discontentment is the primary cause of a midlife crisis. Can a Christian become discontented in marriage if he or she is walking close to Jesus Christ? Not often. The reason is you're able to see things from his perspective. But if you neglect a close relationship with God, you're seeing things through your own selfishness, which breeds discontentment.

Looking at the Downside
Of course, we're not going to sit here and pretend that a good attitude will automatically usher second-decade couples into the Renaissance. During the first ten years of marriage, Joannie Mohler was down on herself. She felt like the only stay-at-home mom in the world as she raised two sons in an empty neighborhood in suburban Seattle. Nagging doubts about not putting her education to use left her unfulfilled, and she hated no longer being a size ten. Consequently, she always had a ready gripe on her lips whenever her husband, Patrick, walked through the front door.

"I'm so fat."

"I never have anyone to talk to."

"Those kids are wearing me out."

"I'm sick of not having any spending money."

After hearing the litany for the fiftieth time, Patrick put his foot down. "You're your own worst enemy," he complained one afternoon. "The only person putting you down is yourself."

That wasn't the response Joannie was fishing for. She wanted Patrick to lift her up, make her feel good about herself. She wanted him to do something about her unhappiness.

"His response irked me," said Joannie. "He wasn't saying what I wanted him to say. I expected him to read my mind and know what my thoughts were. I was hurting, and I felt like a yo-yo. Whether it was a hormonal thing, I don't know, but my hormones were raging at that point."

As her emotional state swung like a playground swing, Patrick swung into action. "There's a marriage conference next weekend at a church about an hour south of us," he said. "I think we should go to it."

"We don't have the money," said Joannie. "Besides, we don't have anyone to watch the kids."

"I've already asked your sister to watch the boys, and she said yes. As for the money, I have some overtime coming in my next paycheck."

Deep down, Joannie didn't want to go because she knew she would have to face some things about herself that would hurt—such as her attitude. She knew she wasn't content.

Despite all her excuses, the Mohlers showed up for the marriage conference. She was right: It *was* painful. "In one session, I had to share these intimate thoughts in a questionnaire," said Joannie. "There I was, sitting in a classroom chair, writing one-liners, and crying. The shades popped up, and I was able to see how much I was missing out by wallowing in self-pity."

The marriage conference, which happened at the Mohlers' eleven-year mark of marriage, took them out of the Dark Ages.

"This is what I have learned," said Joannie. "If there is something bugging me, I have to bring it up. I have to look for the right time to do that, and it's not after 10:00 P.M. We are too tired. A better time might be right after dinner, when I'll be sitting in the living room with Patrick, and the kids are outside. I'll say in a nonthreatening way, 'Pat, this is what I am feeling, and it's not you who is making me feel this way.' I have learned to express myself in a way that will help him understand where I am coming from. If I come at Patrick with a more rational—not emotional—approach, I will connect with him better. But if I react emotionally, he will react defensively, and we will get nowhere."

What We Learned

You've likely caught the drift through the whole book, but it's a fact worth mentioning again. Seeing a counselor and/or attending marriage conferences are often the best investments a couple can make. Mediocre marriages need the boost, and good marriages can always get better. Drop the pride, find a baby-sitter—and go! For dozens of couples we interviewed, those two ways to get a better handle on marriage proved to be the Reformation needed to get out of the Dark Ages.

No Goofing Off

Products of the "Jesus Movement" that swept southern California in the early 1970s, Bryce and Gwen Wickert met at church meetings, and it was in these highly charged settings that the young couple fell in love. "Our relationship was built on a limited perception," remembered Bryce. "We saw each other only in church, song fests, or prophecy meetings. That was good, but we should have done some other things together, like hiking, fishing, or camping with other believers. Our marriage was somewhat unbalanced because we didn't spend enough time discovering what our interests were, what our hobbies were, how we felt about children, my occupation, our finances, or relationships with others."

Gwen said it took more than ten years before she and Bryce even *realized* their marriage was in the Dark Ages. "We went into marriage with our commitment to the Lord, and not much else," she said. "We didn't know one another at all. What we learned is that our commitment to the Lord can—and should—help us in our commitment to each other."

Bryce quoted Proverbs 11:1, "A false balance is abomination to the Lord, but a just weight is his delight" (KJV).

Did you pick up on the word *balance?*

"Our life was unbalanced," said Bryce, "because all we did was attend seminars, teachings, and meetings. Why did we get so involved? Because the world is in disarray and disruptive to marriages. We sought out teaching, which helps you gain greater knowledge, but as the Bible says, knowledge puffs up. I think there is a danger in going to *too* many meetings and church activities."

What We Learned

During their courtship and early years of marriage, Bryce and Gwen never goofed off or did silly things together.

Instead, they were always "spiritually on." Every now and then, they needed to shut down whatever they were doing—be it church, work, or raising children—and enjoy each other. Doing that can recharge a couple for the next season of marriage.

How Quickly the Years Pass

Bob Welch is the father of two sons, thirteen and eleven, and in only five years the older lad will be going off to college. "The way I look at child raising, I see a finish line. This is a forty-eight-hour sale, so I better buy while I can. In just a few years, Sally and I will have all the time in the world for ourselves.

"We have the same philosophy about our kids playing baseball in the backyard: It ruins the lawn. But ten years from now, what will I care about most? That I had a nice lawn or that the kids played baseball with me in the backyard? The lawn loses every time."

With three boys in the house—counting her husband—Sally often feels outnumbered. For example, every fall the guys go out and play football in the mud; she gets the filthy laundry. Bob buys three season tickets to the University of Oregon football games; the boys moan when she wants them to tag along at the mall.

Bob has sought a balance; he makes sure his wife is not overlooked. He knows she enjoys browsing through antique stores, visiting her grandparents' farm in the Willamette Valley, and storming the outlet stores.

We talked earlier about how you can't *change* your spouse to be something he or she isn't. But one point we want to make clear to those in their second decade is that although you can't *make* your spouse change, some amount of change will occur from advancing age and maturity. Call it growth.

Bob Welch said one thing he's seen in twenty years of marriage is that some spouses refuse to let their partner change from the person they married. "It goes back to this natural inclination to have our spouses like everything we like, from hobbies to cereal. For instance, I like to read serious nonfiction, but my wife, Sally, enjoys fiction. I love to go sailing, but she'll go only if it's a beautiful sunny day and she has nothing else to do. I like to invite people spontaneously, but she is more reserved."

No right or wrong answer applies here. The Welches have Christ in common, and that has given them the freedom to be different, to be *themselves.* "Sometimes, I've tried to change my spouse into being what I want her to be, as opposed to appreciating her for who she was," said Bob. "That didn't work."

What are some differences between the first and second decade of love?

Married twenty years, Bernie Knox said the best thing he's noticed is that he and his wife have worked out their differences. "If you have been trying to do that, your marriage will get into a groove," said Bernie. "For Elaine and me, our love has become more comfortable because I know how she will respond. She'll sometimes start a sentence, and I'll finish it. There are not as many surprises the second decade. We trust each other now, which makes me feel comfortable."

Bernie carpools with a fellow who has been married ten

years. They often discuss what lies ahead in the second decade of marriage. "I give him advice," said Bernie, "and while I note that our love is comfortable, I am quick to tell him that it's very important to keep the marriage fresh so you don't take your spouse for granted. That means you should continue to court your wife. That doesn't mean expensive dates. Rather, it means you *emotionally* court your wife by telling her how beautiful she is. For instance, my wife irons my shirts, but only 3 percent of the women in the U.S. do that. [Sounds low to us, Bernie, but we'll take your word for it.] I will compliment her on the fine job of ironing and express my appreciation. I'm very free in doing this because you can never take love for granted. I don't have the emotional highs I had when I was courting Elaine, but I don't have the lows of the first decade, either. I continually stoke the fire, and the way I do that is by letting her know that there is no other woman in the world who can meet my needs like her!"

Sounds like a great weekend at Bernie's!

NOTABLE QUOTABLES

Here are a few more interesting observations on various attitudes in marriage:

- "The goal of marriage isn't happiness, but Christlikeness."

- "Dying to yourself isn't a happy thing. Humility and turning the other cheek aren't, either. But these apply in the day-to-day work that marriage is. When things aren't going right, I'll pray, 'Lord, make it right, give us peace.' It always happens. When I can't pray, the peace never comes."

- "Having the right attitude in marriage starts with choosing to value your spouse. Accept her for who she is and respect her. That's what I've done with my wife. I need to value what God values by granting her respect as a fellow heir" (see 1 Peter 3:7).

- "We became persuaded at how much God is for marriage, and that it's a three-person deal. He promises to put his blessing, power, name, and reputation behind it. If we give ourselves over to him, it will be successful."

- "After our first child was born, we'd ask each other, 'Who do we love more?' It got to the point where it was too hard to keep the right order: God, my husband, then our child. I've learned that having the right order will keep my children happier than if my husband is third."

- "For years my home wasn't a safe place to rest. If I would sit down and relax, my wife would assume I had nothing to do. We finally talked about giving me the freedom to 'get around to it.' If a man can't rest at home, he'll stay at the office and hide or look for other outlets."

- "My ideal goal is to make her feel satisfied, loved, and esteemed. I want every fiber of my being committed to making her wholly satisfied—without asking, 'What's in it for me?' I'm here to serve her, not so that later on tonight she'll pay off. That attitude is very reflective of God who spared not his Son to have a relationship with his bride, the church."

- "When you get married, you make seven vows to love each other: 'for richer, for poorer, for better, for worse, in sickness, and in health, until death do you part.' What you would prefer is that 'death do you part' come long after all the others. The widows I've talked to have said you don't know what you had until you bury your spouse."

• "I'm committed to the journey."

• "I threw a big surprise party for my husband when he made captain for American Airlines. Over a hundred people came to our home, and I presented him with a framed invitation of the party. It was my tribute to him because I know how important it is to show appreciation."

• "Hope. Never lose it. I lost hope in the early years. That's why I despaired so much. I lost hope in God that he could change my situation. When I chose to say, 'I believe by faith you can change this difficult period of life,' then I started to see the small changes grow into bigger ones."

• "Becoming one flesh with your spouse is more a result of leaving and cleaving than sex. The process of cleaving— developing emotional oneness and spiritual bonding—will produce a natural result of physical bonding."

• "I want a wife whose touch on my hand speaks about four chapters of a book—just with that touch. That means more to me than sitting on beachfront property with a bunch of toys, absolutely alone."

• "The acceptance of the fight makes a strong marriage— knowing that the forces of evil are coming against you and that you'll battle for your whole life. A good marriage can't be had without getting a little bloody. I've developed that warrior mentality. I know materialism is that force of evil that greets me each morning. But I'm going to win, because God is for me. I certainly know that lust needs a warrior mentality. Apathy, too. It's a daily fight, but I'm not going to give up. I don't have any alternative if I'm submitting to Jesus Christ."

• "If we're going to be in this thing, we have to make it a joyful deal. We don't want to crawl to the finish line, we want to break the tape and finish well."

- "If I've said something to my husband that's not appropriate, especially in front of the kids, then I make a point of confessing that unkindness. Keeping a short account of miscues has prevented the major problems."

- "Being accountable. Always having someone in your life who knows the condition of your heart, even if you're not at a point of repentance. Knowing there's a person who's praying for you will always play an important role."

- "Tenaciousness. Not just an endurance through bad stuff, but a real desire to make the relationship work."

- "We have to be fun to live with. That's when your mate wants to come home. 'I'd much rather come home and have the house messy and you happy,' my husband said to me when the kids were little."

- "We should be grateful instead of picky and trying to make everything perfect. We need to treasure the times we have together with our children instead of wishing them away."

- "Recognizing the value and fruit that a godly family has. People are drawn to that light. They're desperate to see marriages that work, parents who love their kids, kids who love their parents. We've had people come to the Lord just by spending time with our family."

Where to from Here?

h as marriage met your expectations, or have you experienced some deep disappointments along the way?

That's kind of a loaded question, isn't it? In a left-handed way, we're asking, *If you could change anything about your spouse, what would it be?* To be frank, most of the couples we talked with were quick to mention a few things that bugged them:

- "My husband doesn't talk or help out as much as I need."

- "My wife and I still don't have sex often enough."

- "I thought that by now he'd realize what I need in a godly husband."

Other responses surprised us:

- "I'm disappointed in myself."

- "I know I haven't responded the way I should have."

- "I was so tired those first few years of our marriage that I couldn't have been very understanding."

- "Sometimes I still don't have a clue what I should be doing."

Do you see the difference?

The first set of responses points the finger at the other person, the second set at ourselves.

One thing we learned while writing this book is that as much as we'd like to, we don't have the power to change our spouse, but we can change ourselves. First, however, we have to have the "want-to."

Hopefully, you know that this book wasn't written to change your spouse; it was written to give you some ideas on how you can improve your marriage. Why? So your relationship can move a few steps closer to the Renaissance God wants it to have. Remember when we talked about the "Age of Faith" in chapter 1? The biblical definition of faith is: "being sure of what we hope for and certain of what we do not see" (Heb. 11:1).

If you're in the Dark Ages where the marriage is playing second fiddle to other priorities, remember: Those priorities eventually grow up. Instead of despairing or wondering if they will ever end, we think a better attitude is to realize they *will* end. A Renaissance will occur if you don't give up the faith. Faith in God, faith in each other, and faith in yourself that you can change.

If lasting change needs to occur, it had better happen in the second decade of love—a time when the hopes of the first decade can still come to fruition.

TOP TEN THINGS YOU WILL MISS ABOUT THE KIDS WHEN THEY'RE GONE

10. The opportunity to buy chocolate bars for them by the case

9. The pitter-patter of their stereo headphones

8. The slumber parties

7. Whininess and tattling

6. Curfew

5. All the yard help

4. *Like, um,* and *you know*

3. Reviewing prospective suitors for your daughter

2. The second mortgage you used to pay college tuition

1. Borrowing their car

Questions to Consider

Where do you need to change? Let's take this one spouse at a time. Men first. Grab a pencil. (Go ahead. Find one.) Read through this list of questions and check the boxes that apply.

Set A

☐ 1. Do you try to dominate your wife to stay in control?

☐ 2. Do you always have to win the argument?

☐ 3. When you date your wife, is your goal to have sex at the end of the evening?

☐ 4. Are you doing some things secretly that if your wife found out, she would lose respect for you?

☐ 5. Do you sometimes point the finger at how you were raised as a reason for your poor performance in marriage?

Set B

☐ 6. Do you initiate communication every day?

☐ 7. Do you look for ways to build her self-esteem?

☐ 8. Do you want to improve in the role of spiritual leader?

☐ 9. Is it your goal to have her as your best friend?

☐ 10. Do you know that God didn't give you a wife to meet all your needs?

OK, wives, your turn.

Set A

☐ 1. Is an emphasis on child rearing preventing you from pursuing your husband sexually?

☐ 2. Do you ever withhold sex as a way to "punish" him for his lack of sensitivity?

☐ 3. Do you sometimes point the finger at how you were raised as a reason for your poor performance in marriage?

☐ 4. Are you involved with so many outside activities

that you rarely take time to do the little things to show your husband he's appreciated?

☐ 5. Is sex an obligation more often than not?

Set B

☐ 6. Have you learned how to communicate frustrations or disappointments to your husband in a way he understands (versus expecting him to read your mind)?

☐ 7. Do you still respect your husband?

☐ 8. Are you attempting to encourage and help your husband to be the spiritual leader he wants to be?

☐ 9. Is it your goal to have him as your best friend?

☐ 10. Do you know that God didn't give you a husband to meet all of your needs?

Any questions you checked in Set A pinpoint an area(s) you can start working on. Any questions you left blank in Set B *also* pinpoint an area(s) you can start working on. Notice our advice: *"start* working on." We don't expect you to fix certain areas of your marriage overnight—problems that took years to come to a head. Instead, pick one or two items that need immediate attention. You can talk to your spouse about your newfound resolve to improve your marriage, and then we hope you can use some of the practical ideas we've shared in this book.

Moving toward a Renaissance

By now you've probably discovered which stage your marriage is at. If you haven't, your answers to those ten questions offer more clues. If you checked two or more of the first five questions, you're likely still in the Dark Ages. But if you checked three or more of the second five questions, you're well on your way to a Renaissance. That's great!

You don't need to settle for the Dark Ages in your marriage. Yes, a Reformation is hard work (it may even take years to achieve), but two things are true:

- The couples we interviewed who were still in the Dark Ages knew marriage had to be better than this.

- Couples who had reached a Renaissance had found what they were looking for—and it was *always* worth the price they paid to get there.

These days an excellent marriage does not come without a price; it never has. But things that are worthwhile never come cheap. It is our prayer that you and your spouse will undergo a marital Renaissance that will be as priceless as da Vinci's *Mona Lisa!*

We Need Your Help!

*d*id you struggle your first few years of marriage? Though not all problems can be headed off at the pass, we believe many can. If you'd like to be involved in helping us give some much-needed advice to young couples and you wouldn't mind filling out a short survey, please send your name and address to Greg Johnson, c/o Tyndale House Publishers, Box 80, Wheaton, IL 60189.

While you're at it, we'd like to know if this book helped you or your marriage. Drop us a note. Thanks, and God bless your Renaissance adventure.

Additional titles from Greg Johnson and Mike Yorkey

The Second Decade of Love is also available on Tyndale Living Audio.
0-8423-7434-5

"DADDY'S HOME"   0-8423-0584-X
Interviews with hundreds of dads reveal the most creative ideas and effective approaches on fathering.

FAITHFUL PARENTS, FAITHFUL KIDS   0-8423-1369-9
From these testimonies of Christian parents whose children follow the Lord, you can learn to instill Christian values in your children.

Also by Greg Johnson

IF I COULD ASK GOD *ONE* QUESTION . . .   0-8423-1616-7
These straightforward, scriptural answers to spiritual questions will help teens build a stronger faith.

"IT'S OUR TIME, DAD"   *(New! Fall 1994)*
With Scripture, application, interactive features, rewards, and more, these devotionals will bring dads and kids together.
  20 Fun Lessons from Proverbs   0-8423-1747-3
  20 Fun Lessons from the Life of Jesus   0-8423-1746-5

KEEPING YOUR COOL WHILE SHARING YOUR FAITH
With Susie Shellenberger   0-8423-7036-6
Advice, humor, and encouragement to inspire youth who are reluctant to share their faith with peers.